TRANSITION TO GLIDERS

A FLIGHT TRAINING HANDBOOK
FOR POWER PILOTS

by

THOMAS KNAUFF

Includes FAA Practical Test Standards

TRANSITION TO GLIDERS

A FLIGHT TRAINING HANDBOOK
FOR POWER PILOTS

by

THOMAS KNAUFF

Editors for this edition
Haven Goulding
John Brewer

Drawings by Robert Fitch, James Taylor,
Charlie Weinert, Tom Knauff

Cover photo

Sam Fly dumping water ballast before landing.
Photo by Mark Keene

Rear cover photo
Thomas Knauff & Doris Grove
photo by Tony Firman

TRANSITION TO GLIDERS

A FLIGHT TRAINING HANDBOOK
FOR POWER PILOTS

by

THOMAS KNAUFF

First edition 1984
Second edition 1990
Third edition 1999
Fourth edition 2001
Fifth edition 2008

Library of Congress Catalog Card Number: 83-83439

ISBN 0-9605676-2-3

Printed In the United States of America
by K B Offset, State College, Pennsylvania

Other books by the author:

Glider Basics From First Flight To Solo

Glider Basics From Solo To License

Glider Flight Instructor Manual

Accident Prevention Manual For Glider Pilots

Accident Prevention Manual For Glider Flight Instructors

Off Field Landings

Ridge Soaring The Bald Eagle Ridge

The Glider Flying Handbook

TRANSITION TO GLIDERS

TABLE OF CONTENTS

ABOUT THE AUTHOR

Thomas Knauff is more than a writer; more than a flight instructor. He is one of the world's best soaring pilots. He is the first person in the United States to fly 750 kilometer, 1000 kilometer and 1250 kilometer triangles and the first person to fly 1000 kilometers in a two-place sailplane in the United States.

Tom's list of records include a world record 1647 kilometer (1023 miles) out and return flight, and the first person to break the 200 kilometer per hour barrier on a 300 kilometer out and return speed run at 201.3 kph. He has also flown a 100 km speed triangle at 186 kph. Tom has set five world soaring records and more than four dozen US national records. He has won five nationals chapionships including the United States unlimited soaring championship in 1989. He was the Federal Aviation Administration Eastern Region Flight Instructor of the Year in 1996, and inducted into the Soaring Society Hall of Fame in 1998.

He is one of the premier flight instructors in the world. His glider flight instructor courses are recognized as the best in the country. He was the first in the USA to offer an organized off-field landing course using a motor glider, and the first to offer a competition pilots course.

Tom has written eight books including one of the most successful text books for beginning glider pilots, *Glider Basics From First Flight To Solo*. This book is in its sixth edition, and sold out of the first edition in less than one year. With his unique soaring ability, and an equally unique desire to share with others his profound knowledge of soaring, Tom has provided student glider pilots with a new text book of basic, and advanced knowledge of the sport of soaring flight. *After Solo* will make better, and above all, safer pilots.

Doris Grove

PREFACE

This is the first flight training manual written expressly for the power pilot who is going to transition to gliders. In the past, power pilots were asked to purchase text books that were written for the beginning pilot. These books were filled with information that the power pilot already knew.

It is my hope you find this book filled with worthwhile information without dwelling too much on any subject. If a review of any subject is needed, you will find a bibliography at the end of this book of other texts that you will want to add to your library.

You will discover this sport to be a satisfying, delightful form of flight. Perhaps the kind of flying you have always dreamed of.

Tom Knauff

ACKNOWLEDGEMENTS

Books are written by authors who have knowledge about subjects they are familiar with. Writers subject their "masterpieces" to editors who unmercifully tear ideas and thoughts apart so that you, the reader can understand what the writer means to say. Editors often say that a book would never be, if it wasn't for the writer. They say the original writing is the hardest part. The writer will tell you that the hardest part is making the writer say what is meant. The editors keep thewriter from looking illiterate, and force the writer to make ideas understandable.

The editors of this book have done an outstanding job. You are benefiting from their expert opinions, not only as literary critics, (punctuation and all that stuff), but also from their authority as soaring pilots.

In any work such as this, the final opinion as to how the subject matter is presented must finally fall with the one person who is ultimately responsible: the author. Every attempt was made to ensure the material was presented in accepted, standardized methods as presented by our own FAA, the SSA, and soaring communities around the world. Where differences of opinion existed, the author had to finally choose what he thought best.

I encourage you to write to me care of Ridge Soaring Gliderport, 3523 South Eagle Valley Road, Julian, Pa. 16844, with your comments, suggestions, and criticisms. With your help, the next edition will be even better.

Finally, you must know the behind-the-scenes help I had from Doris Grove, who filled in for me while I spent many hours working on this book, and also did her share of editing, and helping to verbalize the ideas.

Tom Knauff

TRANSITION PILOT FLIGHT TRAINING SYLLABUS

Preparation: Read chapters 1 though 28 of Transition To Gliders.

1st flight
Preflight briefing.
Glider and cockpit preflight including placards and weight & balance limitations.
Ground handing procedures.
Launch procedures including signals.
Instructor demonstrates takeoff & aerotow. Use of trim.
Student attempts aerotow.
Explain/demonstrate release procedure.
Demonstrate speed control using horizon as reference.
Demonstrate yaw string useage.
Practice shallow and medium banked turns.
Thermalling if conditions permit.
Demonstrate TLAR landing technique.
Postflight debriefing.

2nd flight
Preflight briefing.
Demonstrate cockpit pre-takeoff checklist.
Student performs takeoff and aerotow. (Say 200 feet.)
Practice slow flight.
Practice forward and turning stalls. (Six signs of stall.)
Demonstrate reduced 'G'.
Student performs landing pattern and landing.

3rd flight
Preflight briefing.
Student performs takeoff and aerotow. (Say 200 ft.)
Forward and turning stall practice.
Continuous steep turns.
Landing pattern & landing.
Postflight debriefing.

4th flight
Preflight briefing.
Student performs takeoff and aerotow. (Say 200 ft.)
Turning stall practice.
Steep turns.
Slips
Student performs pattern enrty and landing.
Postflight debriefing.

Additional flights as necessary before continuing.

5th flight
Preflight briefing.
Unassisted takeoff. (No wing runner.)
Forward rope break.
Postflight debriefing.

6th & 7th flight
200 ft rope break.
180 turn to landing.
Downwind landing
Postflight debriefing.

8th flight
Student performs entire flight unassisted.

Additional flights as necessary.

Solo

TRANSITION PILOT POST SOLO TRAINING SYLLABUS

Read remainder of Trnsition To Gliders,
and The Glider Flying Handbook.

1st flight
Preflight briefing.
Unassisted takeoff.
CFI demonstrates and student performs
  boxing the wake.
CFI demonstrates and student performs
  benign spiral mode.
Student performs right hand landing
  pattern and landing.
Postflight debriefing.

2nd flight
Preflight briefing.
Student performs boxing the propwash.
CFI demonstrates, student performs
  cross-controlled stalls.
Practice steep 720 degree turns.
Accuracy pattern and landing into a
  prescribed zone without the use of the
  altimeter.
Postflight debriefing.

3rd flight
Preflight briefing.
Student performs low tow position
  during aerotow.
Demonstrate spin entry and recovery.
Demonstrate spiral dive entry and
  recovery.
CFI sets up faulty approach
Postflight debriefing.

4th flight.
Preflight briefing.
Review and perform aerotow signals.
CFI demonstrates, student performs deep
  stalls.
Faulty approach followed by downwind
  landing.
Postflight debriefing.

5th flight
Preflight briefing.
Flight test recommendation flgiht.
Review all flight test maneuvers.
Simulated off-field landing, preferably at
  a different site.
Postflight debriefing.

6th flight
Preflight briefing.
Review flgiht test maneuvers.
Downwind landing into specified zone.
Postflight debriefing.

Additional dual flights when conditions
permit:

Thermalling, ridge soaring, wave
  soaring.
Solo flight in single place glider.
Chandelles, Lazy eghts.
ABC, Bronze badge requirements.

CHAPTER 1

WHAT THE FAR'S SAY

Part 61.87 of the FAR's cover solo flight. Your instructor will review part 91 (flight rules) Part 830 (accident reporting) and the following procedures and operations:

1. Proper flight preparation procedures, including preflight planning, preparation, aircraft systems, and, if appropriate, powerplant operations.
2. Taxiing or surface operations, including run-ups, if applicable.
3. Launches, including normal and crosswind.
4. Straight and level flight, and turns in both directions, if applicable.
5. Airport traffic patterns, including entry procedures.
6. Collision avoidance, wind shear avoidance, and wake turbulence avoidance.
7. Descents with and without turns using high and low drag configurations.
8. Flight at various airspeeds.
9. Emergency procedures and equipment malfunctions.
10. Ground reference maneuvers, if applicable.
11. Inspection of towline rigging and review of signals and release procedures, if applicable.
12. Aerotow, ground tow, or self-launch procedures.
13. Procedures for disassembly and assembly of the glider.
14. Stall entry, stall, and stall recovery.
15. Straight glides, turns, and spirals.
16. Landings, including normal and crosswind.
17. Slips to a landing.
18. Procedures and techniques for thermalling.
19. Emergency operations, including towline break procedures.

It is not common for student pilots to be permitted to fly cross country in gliders, but provisions are made in part 61.93.

To meet the requirements for the private glider flight test, you will need endorsements for all of the above, plus the items in 61.105:

1. Applicable Federal Aviation Regulations of this chapter that relate to private pilot privileges, limitations, and flight operations.
2. Accident reporting requirements of the National Transportation Safety Board.
3. Use of the applicable portions of the "Aeronautical Information Manual" and FAA advisory circulars.
4. Use of aeronautical charts for VFR navigation using pilotage, dead reckoning, and navigation systems.
5. Radio communication procedures.

6. Recognition of critical weather situations from the ground and in flight, wind shear avoidance, and the procurement and use of aeronautical weather reports and forecasts.
7. Safe and efficient operation of aircraft, including collision avoidance, and recognition and avoidance of wake turbulence.
8. Effects of density altitude on takeoff and climb performance.
9. Weight and balance computations.
10. Principles of aerodynamics, power plants, and aircraft systems.
11. Stall awareness, spin entry, spins, and spin recovery techniques for the airplane and glider category ratings.
12. Aeronautical decision making and judgment.
13. Preflight action that includes - (i) How to obtain information on runway lengths at airports of intended use, data on takeoff and landing distances, weather reports and forecasts, and fuel requirements; and (ii) How to plan for alternatives if the planned flight cannot be completed or delays are encountered.

Part 61.107 lists the flight instruction required to be logged from an authorized flight instructor:

1. Preflight preparations.
2. Preflight procedures.
3. Airport and gliderport operations.
4. Launches and landings.
5. Performance speeds.
6. Soaring techniques.
7. Performance maneuvers.
8. Navigations.
9. Slow flight and stalls.
10. Emergency operations.
11. Postflight procedures.

As a rated power pilot, you need forty hours of combined flight time in heavier-than-air aircraft, and three hours of flight training in a glider in the above listed procedures and operations. This needs to be with an authorized flight instructor within the preceding 60 days prior to the test. Your flight time must include 10 solo flights in a glider and 3 flights with a flight instructor in preparation for the flight test.

THE COMMERCIAL GLIDER RATING

If you have a commercial power plane rating, you might elect to earn the commercial glider rating as well. The requirements are very similar to the private glider rating, although you need to show additional proficiency.

You need to know the FARs pertaining to commercial operations, and be able to stop within a 100 foot zone instead of the 200 foot zone required by the private flight test.

In addition, you need 200 hours of pilot time in heavier-than-air aircraft, including 20 glider flights as pilot in command.

THE FAA WRITTEN TEST

No written test is required if you hold a fixed wing rating and are applying for a glider rating equal to or less than your power rating. If you hold a helicopter rating and no fixed wing rating, you will be required to take the written test unless you hold a commercial helicopter rating and are obtaining a commercial glider rating. The commercial oral and flight test will, of course, be more demanding than the private flight test.

THE FLIGHT TEST STANDARDS

FAA-S-8081-22 describes the FAA Flight Test Standards that will be used when you take your flight test. The FARs require you to receive instruction and demonstrate competency in all pilot operations listed in Part 61 of the regulations.

As a licensed power pilot, you may find the glider flight instructor taking for granted that you know more than you really do. For your own good, and to save the embarrassment of failing a flight test, be sure to review the flight test standards and the FAR requirements. Make certain all areas have been covered, and the appropriate log book endorsements have been made.

This does not mean it is required to repeat flight training just to fill up your log book. If you are able to perform any flight maneuver to the standards required by the flight test guide, well and good.

Long ago, commercially rated glider pilots were able to give flight instruction. The FAA passed new regulations establishing glider flight instructor ratings. In the good ol' days, power pilots were sometimes permitted to solo gliders with only a couple of dual flights, and in some cases were soloed with only a ground briefing and no dual flights! I'd like to believe those days are over, but just recently I was told of a power transition pilot who was soloed with only two dual flights.

A transition glider course should have a minimum of eight to ten dual flights for a current, proficient power pilot to solo a glider.

The flight test includes an oral quiz on the following subjects:

1. PREFLIGHT PREPARATION, including documents, weight and balance, weather, flight instruments, glider assembly, and performance limitations.

2. GROUND OPERATIONS, including ground handling, visual inspection, and pre-takeoff check.

3. GLIDER LAUNCHES AND TOWS, including signals, crosswind takeoffs, slack line, boxing the wake, tow release, and abnormal procedures.

4. IN-FLIGHT MANEUVERS, including straight flight, turns, steep turns, recovery from unusual attitudes, maneuvering at minimum controllable airspeeds and stall recognition and recoveries.

5. PERFORMANCE SPEEDS, including best glide speed, minimum sink speed, and speed to fly.

6. SOARING TECHNIQUES, including thermalling, ridge soaring, wave soaring, and mountain soaring.

7. APPROACHES AND LANDINGS, including traffic patterns, normal and crosswind landings, slips to landing, downwind landings, and simulated off-field landings.

CHAPTER 2

HOW A GLIDER FLIES
A REVIEW OF AERODYNAMICS

Many power pilots are very experienced and may even be flight instructors. However, there are some who have not looked at a textbook in a long time. This chapter will serve as a memory jogger, and perhaps cause you to dig out some of those textbooks from long ago.

The last pages of this book include a bibliography of recommended textbooks you may want to add to your library. Some deal with the basics of flight, while others are quite technical. It is important to develop a small library of references if you are going to become an expert glider pilot.

Many glider pilots are extraordinarily good pilots. They have to be if they are going to win soaring competitions or set records for speed or distance. Sloppy flying detracts from the performance of a sleek, modern sailplane. To fly one of these beauties to their ultimate performance requires a thorough understanding of how they work and how to fly them perfectly.

THE CONTROLS

The elevator serves the same purpose as a power plane, controlling the angle of attack of the wing, and therefore the airspeed. It is especially important to understand the elevator is not used for the up and down control. The exception is relatively small, temporary changes in altitude as the glider is slowed from high airspeeds.

The ailerons control the bank angle and thus the rate of turn. In a glider, you will notice a greater amount of aileron drag or adverse yaw when the ailerons are used.

The rudder is used to counteract aileron drag, the same as a power plane. Most power pilots have some difficulty using enough rudder to offset the aileron drag. The wings of a glider are very long, and the ailerons have a lot of leverage compared to power planes. In addition, many power planes have coupled controls so the rudder moves when the pilot moves the ailerons. The effect of aileron drag is more pronounced in gliders.

People have a tendency to use the same amount of *pressure* on the rudder pedals as they use to deflect the ailerons. The rudder requires much more pressure to cause the movement necessary. On your first glider flight, you will try several turn entries and recoveries to get the feel of the ailerons and rudder.

One new instrument is the yaw string. A yaw string is a short piece of yarn fastened to the canopy in direct view of the pilot. The yaw string serves the same purpose as the slip-skid indicator in a power plane. It shows when the pilot used the controls incorrectly and allowed the aircraft to fly uncoordinated. The yaw string is very quick to show your errors: much quicker than a slip-skid indicator.

The yaw string indicates "backwards" from a slip-skid indicator. You may find it easiest to remember which rudder to push to straighten the yaw string by thinking of the piece of tape holding the yaw string as the ball in a slip-skid indicator. Simply "step on the ball" to correct for an off-center yaw string.

Question - Who invented the yaw string? Answer — Wilbur Wright.

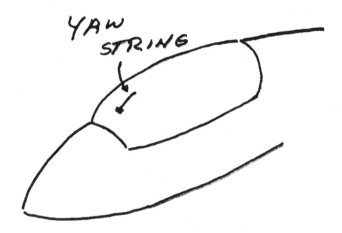

FLAPS

If the glider has flaps, they serve the same purpose as on a power plane; to increase drag to control the glide slope during landing, and to provide a slower stall speed. Because flaps increase the lift the wing produces (with a penalty of increased drag and an increased sink rate), glider pilots also use them to reduce the diameter of the circle while thermalling.

On many gliders, the flaps can be set to a negative, or reflexed setting for better performance during high-speed cruising. The negative setting is used to effectively reduce the wing area, and increase the wing loading, which improves performance at high speeds.

DIVE BRAKE

The one control that is different from most power planes is the dive brake or spoiler. A glider pilot only gets one chance to land. The basic idea is to enter the landing pattern at an altitude that is too high, and "spoil off" excess altitude with the spoilers or dive brakes.

Spoilers and dive brakes are different. Spoilers are set well forward on the airfoil and "spoil" the airflow when deployed. At the same time, spoilers also produce a small amount of drag. The problem with spoilers is that they are positioned at a critical part of the airfoil and spoil some performance all of the time.

Dive brakes are positioned well back on the wing, usually behind the spar line. They are much larger than spoilers. Their primary function is to produce drag. They also disrupt the airflow, causing a small amount of spoiling effect.

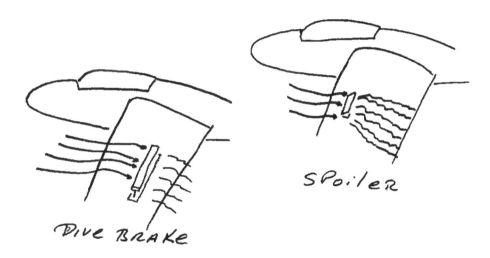

Spoilers are no longer used on modern gliders, but the name "dive brake" conjures up effects that do not occur. Dive brakes do not "brake" you or "dive" you.

It's too bad we don't call both of these devices "spoilers" because they both spoil off excess altitude.

WHEEL BRAKE

Most gliders have a wheel brake, and the actuating mechanism is often at the end of the spoiler travel or sometimes on a lever mounted on the control stick. A few gliders have a foot operated brake lever on the floor.

USING THE CONTROLS ON YOUR FIRST FLIGHT

It is common for power pilots to have difficulty with aero-tow because they are not used to the amount of rudder required to offset aileron drag. The glider will seem to slide back and forth across the centerline of the tow plane.

You will do better on the second flight after you try the following experiment:

After release from tow, try using the ailerons by themselves, making no attempt to coordinate with the rudder. The resulting aileron drag effect is quite dramatic. The instant you apply aileron, the nose of the glider swings in the opposite direction. This is caused by aileron drag. During the aero-tow, when you applied aileron and the nose began to yaw in the opposite direction, your brain might interpret this as not having applied enough aileron! Some might consider the resulting large aileron movements as "overcontrolling." However, the problem is really *under-controlling* of the rudder.

Now you know why you were having so much difficulty on tow! At first, keep the control motions gentle until you get used to the coordination. Course, crisp, control inputs are much more difficult to coordinate than gentle ones.

HOW A GLIDER FLIES — A REVIEW

It should be obvious to advanced students and instructors, for clarity and simplicity, "The Whole Story" sometimes is not given. The student is given what he or she needs to know — when they need to know it. An explanation of the dynamics and physics making flight possible becomes so complicated, if an elaborate explanation is given, a basic text book becomes too complicated.

Bookstores, libraries, and the FAA have several excellent texts on aerodynamics for the person who wishes to study more advanced theories of flight.

The airflow speeds up over the curved upper surface of the wing causing a decreased pressure on the top surface while the air striking the lower surface of the wing causes a higher pressure. The combination of unequal air pressures and deflected airflow create an upward force called "lift."

In 1687 an Englishman, Sir Isaac Newton, observed that "For every action there is an equal and opposite reaction."

This principle applies to the wing as it passes through the air. As the airflow passes over the wing, it is deflected downward. Thus, this downward deflection of the airflow has an "equal and opposite reaction" of pushing, or lifting the wing upward.

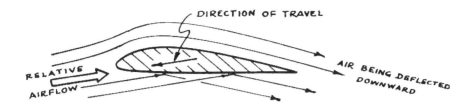

This "deflected air" principle plays a very large role in the aerodynamic theory of lift produced by an airfoil.

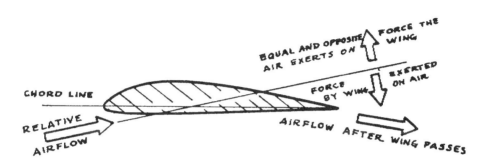

The amount of lift a wing produces is a function of the mass of the air passing over the wing, and the angle of attack of the wing to the airflow. Remember, *angle of attack is the angle at which the relative airflow meets the wing chord line.*

The greater the mass of air flowing past the wing, the more lift produced. Also, the greater the angle of attack, the more lift produced — up to a point.

At high speed where a larger mass of air passes over the wing, a very small angle of attack is needed to deflect the air sufficiently to produce the desired amount of lift.

(See drawing next page)

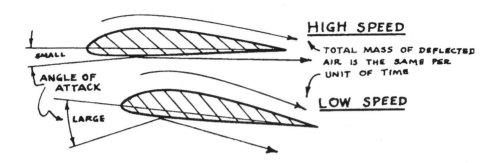

At slow speeds, less air flows over the wing, and a larger angle of attack is needed to deflect the air enough to create the desired amount of lift.

The angle of attack for different airspeeds must be such that the force of deflection of the air mass is equal to the amount of lift needed.

If an aircraft's speed is too slow, the angle of attack required will be so large the airflow can no longer follow the upper curvature of the wing. This results in the airflow separating into a turbulent stream of air. The wing stalls and insufficient lift is produced to maintain normal flight.

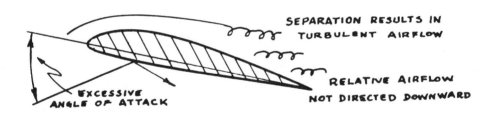

The minimum angle of attack at which airflow separates, and the wing stalls, is called the *critical angle of attack*. On most glider airfoils, this critical angle of attack is 16 to 18 degrees.

AILERONS, ELEVATOR AND RUDDER

When a control surface is moved, the angle of attack is changed. The air is more or less deflected, which causes more or less lift for that part of the airfoil.

Any time a control surface is moved, the relative angle of attack is changed. Anytime angle of attack is changed, not only is lift affected, but speed and drag change as well.

10

```
┌─────────────────────────────────────────────────┐
│                                                   │
│        INCREASING THE ANGLE OF ATTACK:            │
│                                                   │
│            1. INCREASES LIFT                      │
│            2. INCREASES DRAG                      │
│            3. DECREASES SPEED                      │
│                                                   │
└─────────────────────────────────────────────────┘
```

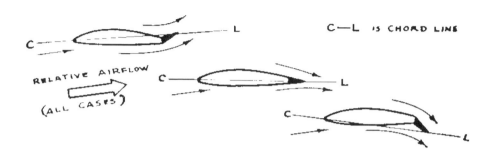

It is important to use the controls sparingly when you are trying to squeeze the maximum performance from the glider. Moving the controls excessively causes unnecessary drag, which hurts the glider's performance.

DRAG

Three kinds of drag act on an aircraft; parasite drag, induced drag, and interference drag.

PARASITIC DRAG is created by air moving against the skin of an aircraft. The shape of an aircraft is streamlined as much as possible, and the skin is smooth in order to decrease parasite drag to a minimum.

INDUCED DRAG is caused by the wing producing lift. As the wing deflects air downward, the total resulting lift is not all exactly vertical. Some is tilted rearward, causing a rearward drag force. The larger the angle of attack, the larger the rearward drag force.

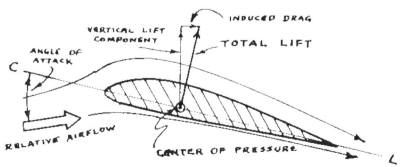

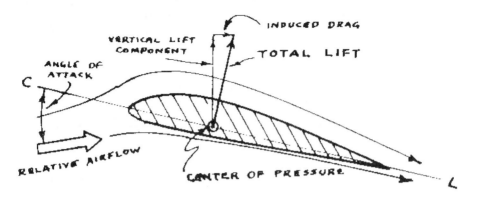

INTERFERENCE DRAG is disrupted airflow at the junction of the wing and fuselage or the tail surfaces.

STABILITY

In order to make an aircraft safe and easy to fly, designers build the aircraft to be as nearly stable as possible. After all, air is pretty thin stuff, and a free flying object might revolve or move about in an uncontrolled manner if it were not for stability.

An aircraft is free to revolve about three axes. Each axis is perpendicular to the other two, and all three intersect at the aircraft's *center of gravity*, or C.G.

Center of Gravity is the point around which the aircraft's weight is evenly distributed or balanced.

The axis which extends through the fuselage from nose to tail is the longitudinal axis. An aircraft rolls about the longitudinal axis by use of the ailerons.

The axis that extends from wingtip to wingtip is called the lateral axis. An aircraft pitches about the lateral axis by use of the elevator.

The axis which passes vertically through the fuselage at the center of gravity is the vertical axis. The aircraft yaws about the vertical axis when the rudder is moved.

An unstable aircraft would require the pilot to continuously move all of the controls to maintain balance, and would therefore be difficult to fly.

Stability means the ability of an aircraft to return to a normal flight attitude if it is disturbed by an outside force.

12

An aircraft is made to be stable as the result of the weathervaning effect of the vertical stabilizer, the balancing act of the CG, the center of pressure, the downward force on the horizontal stabilizer, and finally, the dihedral of the wing.

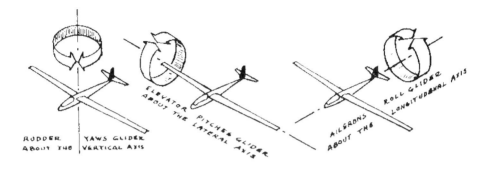

RUDDER | YAWS GLIDER
ABOUT THE | VERTICAL AXIS

ELEVATOR ABOUT THE LATERAL PITCHES GLIDER AXIS

AILERONS ABOUT THE ROLL GLIDER LONGITUDINAL AXIS

When an aircraft is banked, it tends to sideslip (fall sideways) towards the lowered wing.

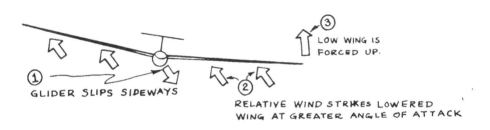

① GLIDER SLIPS SIDEWAYS

② RELATIVE WIND STRIKES LOWERED WING AT GREATER ANGLE OF ATTACK

③ LOW WING IS FORCED UP.

Since the wings have dihedral, airflow in the resulting sideslip strikes the lower wing at a higher angle of attack, producing more lift than the high wing, which tends to restore the aircraft to level flight.

13

To give you an idea of how complicated this all can get, consider the fact that the fuselage and center of gravity are usually well below the wing, which causes a pendulum affect to occur. Also, the vertical stabilizer being above the fuselage and wing causes a corrective rolling motion during a sideslip.

FREE DIRECTIONAL OSCILLATIONS

Most aircraft respond to a disturbance, such as a gust, in a combined rolling-yawing oscillation. The rolling motion is purposely phased to precede the yawing motion. Furthermore, the yawing motion, further, is not too significant, but the roll is often quite noticeable.

When the aircraft rolls back toward level flight due to its built-in roll stability, it rolls too far, overshoots level and begins to sideslip the opposite direction.

If a designer tries to overcome this rolling oscillation, another evil — spiral instability, becomes a problem.

The designer then has a choice of two evils, and must compromise the design. Most aircraft show a mild tendency to spiral. As a pilot, you will only notice it by the fact the aircraft cannot be flown "hands-off" indefinitely.

The designer must not build too much stability into the design. For instance, an overly stable aircraft would be very difficult to turn because it would have too strong a tendency to roll level when the pilot desired to turn the aircraft.

SPIRAL INSTABILITY

What all this boils down to is an aircraft is not very stable in roll. As soon as a moderate bank angle is attained, the aircraft is apt to remain in the resulting spiral. In fact, most aircraft if left on their own will eventually enter a turn. The turn will gradually become steeper and tighter, and the nose will drop. Many aircraft thus end up in a spiral dive.

What happens is this: Suppose an aircraft is flying straight and level. The pilot's hands and feet are off the controls. A gust causes the right wing to go down, resulting in a slight side-slip to the right. The dihedral of the wings tries to pick up the right wing, but the cross flow of air is acting on the entire aircraft. The cross flow of air strikes the tail and fuselage, and the tail causes a yawing motion toward the lowered wing. This yawing force in most aircraft is stronger than what the dihedral is able to overcome, and so the aircraft shows a distinct tendency to increase the bank angle .

This process continues over and over again, causing the turn to become steeper and steeper. The "G" loads due to centrifugal force build up, causing the nose to drop and airspeed to increase.

14

The pilot, of course, prevents a spiral from happening with early, small control corrections that become nearly subconscious, just as an automobile driver prevents the car from falling off the edge of the road by subconscious movements of the steering wheel.

If you want to know more about how an aircraft works, recommended books include *Stick and Rudder* by Wolfgang Langewiesche, *The Flight Training Handbook* by the FAA, and *Understanding Gliding* by Derek Piggott. It is important to fully understand the aircraft you are flying. The information you read here will give you a starting point from which to measure your sailplane's flying characteristics against others, and to better understand what your aircraft wants to do and why.

```
┌─────────────────────────────┐
│        CHAPTER 3            │
│                            │
│     INSTRUMENTATION        │
└─────────────────────────────┘
```

CHAPTER 3

INSTRUMENTATION

A typical sailplane will have at least the following instrumentation:

1. Altimeter
2. Airspeed Indicator
3. Mechanical Variometer
4. Electrical Variometer
5. Audio
6. Compass
7. Yaw String

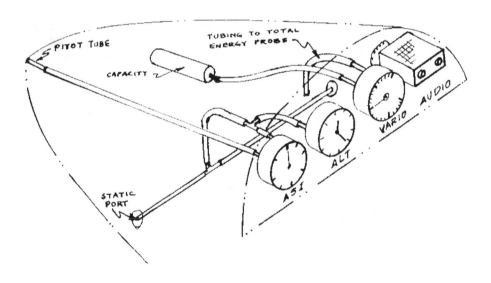

ALTIMETER

It is possible to set the altimeter at "0" or to the field elevation above sea level (MSL, or *Mean Sea Level*). FAR Part 91.121 requires altimeters to be set at field elevation. A "0" setting might be considered OK for early training flights or if you are flying in a flat area like Iowa or Kansas, but it is wise to get used to a field elevation setting so you get used to the mental gymnastics required when flying cross country in undulating or mountainous terrain.

People tend to stick with whatever system they are introduced to and resist any changes. This is one of the reasons we resist learning the metric system or using a 24 hour clock. If you start with a "0" altimeter setting, you may have difficulty at some later time when it will be important to be proficient using the more practical, field elevation. If you begin your training using field elevation on the altimeter, you will have no problems later.

The interior of a glider is usually at a lower pressure than the outside of the aircraft, and many altimeters are vented only to the cockpit pressure. This results in a slightly erroneous reading which usually is insignificant. A more accurate altimeter will be vented to a proper static port.

AIRSPEED INDICATOR

The airspeed indicator is a very sensitive instrument measuring the differential pressure between pitot pressure and static pressure. It indicates the airspeed the glider is moving through the air (not the speed along the ground).

The instrument can be calibrated in several different speed indications. Knots, miles per hour, and kilometers per hour are the most common. In aviation, knots are convenient because sectional charts are marked in degrees and seconds (one minute of latitude is approximately one nautical mile).

If the variometer is also calibrated in knots, simply divide the airspeed in knots by the rate of sink in knots, to determine the L/D, or glide ratio.

The airspeed indicator has several colored markings:

> The white sector is the speed flaps may be used.
> The green sector is the normal operating range.
> The yellow sector is permitted only in calm air.
> The red line is the never-exceed speed.

Some airspeed indicators in gliders have a small yellow triangle at the minimum recommended landing pattern airspeed, which also corresponds to the maximum glide speed. This "bug speed" would only apply at the aircraft's minimum weight. Heavier weights will require higher airspeeds. Note: When landing, you should add 1/2 of any wind to this speed plus a factor for turbulence or gusts.)

VARIOMETER

The variometer is essential for modern soaring flight. It is a very sensitive rate of climb instrument showing if the glider is climbing or descending, and how fast. The variometer can be calibrated in knots, feet per minute, or meters per second.

Basic variometers work by detecting a rate of airflow between a capacity and a static source. As the glider climbs, the air inside the capacity expands and flows out through the instrument. When the glider descends, the air flows into the flask. The rate which this air flows causes the variometer needle to deflect the appropriate amount.

Electric variometers work on the principle of air flowing past thermistors which causes differential cooling and requires differential voltage to keep the thermistors at a constant temperature. Electric variometers tend to be much quicker than mechanical variometers, with a 1 1/2 second delay being average. Conversly, a normal mechanical variometer has double the delay or even worse.

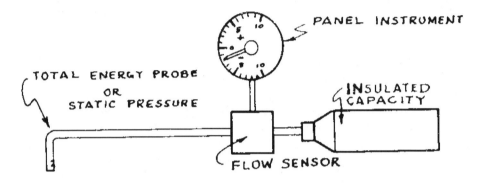

TOTAL ENERGY PROBE

A variometer installed as described will work just fine, showing when the glider climbs and descends. The problem with this simple system is if the pilot pulls the control stick back, the glider converts any extra airspeed (kinetic energy) into altitude (potential energy) and the variometer will show the resulting climb. These pilot induced climbs and descents are commonly called "stick thermals". These stick thermals can be misleading when the pilot is trying to find thermal lift.

Stick thermals can be cancelled out by installing a total energy device. The most common of these is a total energy probe. A total energy probe is usually a long bent tube with slots or tiny holes on the downstream side, and mounted on the leading edge of the vertical stabilizer.

A total energy (T.E) probe produces a very small calibrated suction on the static side of the variometer system. This suction varies with airspeed, and therefore cancels out changes in airspeed

There are other ways to produce total energy, but the T.E. probe is simple, effective and inexpensive. Electric variometers can perform this task electronically.

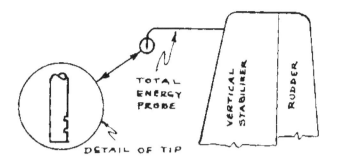

DETAIL OF TIP

TOTAL ENERGY PROBE

VERTICAL STABILIZER

RUDDER

NETTO

It is possible to subtract the glider's sink rate at all speeds so the variometer shows only what the air mass surrounding the glider is doing. This is called a "netto" variometer. A netto variometer is quite useful while cruising from one thermal to the next at high speed.

A netto variometer measures the air the glider is flying through to help the pilot decide if any exisiting lift is worth stopping for, or if it might be better to press on to the next area of lift. An accurate netto indication is very difficult to achieve.

RELATIVE NETTO

Relative netto indicates what the glider's climb rate would be if the glider slowed to climbing speed,and is sometimes called "Super Netto."

AUDIO

An important option is an audio device for the variometer. This can be installed on either a mechanical or electric variometer. The audio provides an audible sound when the variometer needle deflects. The typical climb tone is a broken beep-beep-beep that increases in pitch and frequency as the climb rate improves. The descending sound is a steady tone that decreases in pitch as the sink rate increases.

The variometer can be equipped with a speed-to-fly ring.

More on that later. Competition pilots will equip their gliders with the newest electronic gadgetry. Audio speed-to-fly directors and GPS based flight computers are very useful in reducing the workload on competition pilots. Pilots can then concentrate on flying accurately, while watching outside the glider for clues as to where the next best lift can be found.

Schempp-Hirth Discus
Courtesy Schempp-Hirth Sailplanes

CHAPTER 4

GROUND HANDLING

Sailplanes are built to be light in weight but strong as well. Designers must take into consideration the loads put on a sailplane during ground handling.

Especially weak areas include all control surfaces, the trailing edge of the wing, and all of the fabric and skin of the aircraft. The nose of the fuselage of many sailplanes is thin metal or fiberglass, so no pressure should be put on this area. Wing tip wheels should not be used to pull the glider, or tie it down.

Places which are usually strong enough for handling include special handling bars or handles, wing tips, the leading edge of the wing, and wing struts. The glider should not be moved forward or backwards using the wing tips if the ground is soft or if a great effort is required. Pulling the glider by the wing tips can cause damage to the wing root area, or to the fuselage connections.

Use special care when pushing some gliders backwards. If the elevator is very close to the ground, it can be damaged. Be sure to lift the tail, tie the stick back or pull the trim full back to hold the elevator up when pushing these gliders backwards.

NEVER leave a canopy open and unattended. If the canopy falls or the wind blows it shut, it may crack. While preflighting the exterior of the glider, be sure to close and lock the canopy.

On gliders with a sliding glass window in the canopy, do not lift up or push down on the window opening. The plastic slide rails are very fragile and expensive, plus you can easily break the canopy. Open a canopy by lifting on the frame or other strong structure.

You will be shown how to properly tie down the sailplane and lock the controls for protection from wind damage.

Never leave the sailplane unattended if it is not tied down. Unexpected gusts on otherwise calm days have destroyed sailplanes while helpless onlookers watched in horror!

The minimum effort on reasonably calm days is to place an old tire or other weight on the upwind wing tip, while the glider is positioned with it's nose pointed across the wind.

The last pilot in command of the glider is always responsible for it's security.

When towing a glider with a vehicle, the towrope should be more than 1/2 wingspan, and there should be at least a person at each wing tip. If there are windy conditions or the glider is being towed downhill, more people should be placed on the nose and tail of the glider. In severe conditions, a pilot may also have to be seated in the glider to help control it while being towed. In strong conditions, it may be wise to leave the glider tied down rather than attempting to move it. Always have an adequate number of people.

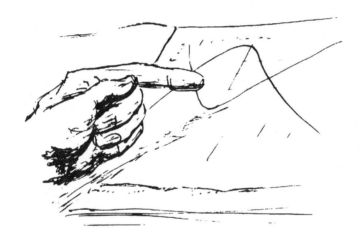

CHAPTER 5

PREFLIGHT

Inspecting the glider before flight is commonly called a preflight inspection. The Federal Aviation Administration (FAA) considers all preparations for flight to be included in a preflight inspection Examples include checking weather conditions, reviewing maps for a cross country flight, and other matters not involving the actual checking of the aircraft. The FAA considers the inspection of the aircraft to be a "Line Inspection". For the purposes of this manual, we will use the generic term, "preflight", to mean the inspection of the glider only. However, you must understand there are many other preflight matters to be concerned about for safe flight preparation.

The aircraft flight manual will specify those items that must be checked on a preflight inspection. Your instructor will show you how to preflight the particular sailplane you are going to use in your training program. The following generalizations apply to all sailplanes.

You are inspecting the sailplane for three reasons:

1. Is it is assembled properly?

2. Is it is in good condition with no hidden damage?

3. Is it is legal to fly?

The Federal Government, through the F.A.A, has given glider pilots special permission to assemble and disassemble their sailplanes. A power pilot is not allowed to remove a wing (only a licensed aircraft mechanic is permitted to do this). The FAA recognizes the special nature of soaring and allows us to do what the power pilot may not. (See Federal Aviation Regulation Part 43.)

This privilege carries with it the responsibility to be sure the pilot is competent to perform an assembly and disassembly, and also recognize when a sailplane has not been assembled properly by someone else.

Read the aircraft flight manual carefully. It will explain how to assemble the sailplane and what important items to inspect during the preflight.

An aircraft must have certain documents to meet federal regulations. You can remember these required documents by knowing that all aircraft must have an OAR on board.

O — Operating limitations in the form of the owners manual or placards including weight and balance data.

A — Airworthiness Certificate.

R — Registration Certificate.

Another common checklist is ARROW, which includes Weight and balance information and Radio station license if the aircraft has a radio.

The airworthiness certificate is issued to the aircraft when it was new. The certificate states this type of aircraft is licensed in a particular category (normal, utility, aerobatic). It is not a certificate to show this particular aircraft is airworthy. The airworthiness certificate never expires.

The registration certificate shows who owns the aircraft, and is only changed when ownership changes.

HIDDEN DAMAGE

A damaged aircraft may be unsafe to fly. Damage can be caused by landing hard, handling the glider improperly, exceeding the structural limits by flying too fast, using the controls improperly, or something bumping into it on the ground.

Pay particular attention to wrinkled or cracked skin near the landing gear and the tail forward of the vertical stabilizer (hard landing or ground loop) or on the wing and tail surfaces (excessive in-flight maneuvering). Excessive use of the controls at high speeds might show up as bent or cracked hinge attach points on the ailerons, rudder or elevator. Damaged dive brake hinges or a slightly bent dive brake might indicate use at excessive speeds.

Loose rivets (popped rivets) or wrinkled metal between the rivets, caused by overstressing a part of the glider, would show possible internal damage. Pay close attention to the space between the rivets for evidence of buckling of the metal, which may indicate overstressing.

Damage also can occur when the sailplane is bumped into something or when someone falls against the aircraft.

CRITTERS

The inside of an aircraft makes a great home for porcupines, skunks, other furry animals, snakes, hornets and wasps! Inspect the inside of the fuselage and the air vent. The pitot tube seems to be a great home for spiders. Mice chew on seat belts for the salt left by human perspiration, and also chew electrical wiring insulation.

MISCELLANEOUS

The airspeed indicator and variometer instruments should read '0', the glass face unbroken, and the altimeter should be able to be adjusted to the field elevation with a proper barometric setting in the window of the altimeter.

The release hook should be clean and in good condition. The backward release spring should have obvious tension. Inspect the area around the release mechanism for signs of overstressing.

The spaces under and behind the seat cushions should be checked for ballast weights. Remove any not needed. Secure or remove any loose objects.

You are responsible for the condition of the tow rope.

If you find any discrepancy, bring it to the attention of your flight instructor.

PREFLIGHT CHECKLIST

There are many items to be checked on a preflight inspection. It is easy to overlook or forget an item. You may be distracted while performing the preflight inspection or you may allow yourself to be rushed and not perform a complete inspection. Many accidents could have been prevented by the pilot noticing some problem during a thorough preflight inspection.

Some sailplanes can have a critical item that <u>must</u> be checked before flight which only apply to that particular type of sailplane.

The manufacturer is required to provide a written preflight checklist. Using this checklist on every preflight is the best way to perform a complete, thorough preflight inspection. By using a written checklist, the pilot is ensured of checking all important items. Most gliders keep the written checklist on board. Use it on every preflight inspection! If the glider does not have a written checklist on board, ask for the flight manual and use the factory preflight checklist. It is common to add additional items to the checklist.

POSITIVE CONTROL CHECK

One common accident is for a glider pilot to take off with one of the controls not connected. During the preflight inspection, you will be shown how to perform a positive control check. This is done by having one person hold a control surface while another puts pressure, first one way then the other, on the entire control actuating mechanism by attempting to move the control from inside the cockpit with the control stick or other control handle. If a control is not connected properly, a looseness would be felt. Don't be so aggressive with the positive control check that you damage the glider!

WEIGHT AND BALANCE

If the glider is to fly properly, it must be within correct weight and balance limits. It must balance properly. Each aircraft has a weight and balance sheet in its records. Most gliders also have a placard in the cockpit applying in most, but not all, situations. If the placard does not cover your situation, you will have to refer to the weight and balance sheet.

The placard on some gliders, such as the Schweizer 2-33, can be confusing and easily misinterpreted. Be sure an instructor reviews the weight and balance data on any glider you are not familiar.

In small power planes, the pilot and passengers sit very near the C.G. and therefore don't influence the C.G. location very much. In a glider, the pilot and passengers sit well in front of the C.G. and therefore may greatly effect the C.G. location.

THE WALK AROUND INSPECTION

Suppose you preflight the glider, fly, land and take a break. A short time later you return and find the glider has not been flown during your absence.

You may not need to do a complete preflight inspection, but you should walk around the glider looking for any damage or for control locks installed to prevent wind damage during your absence. Another positive control check would be a good idea. If there is any possibility that someone may have been probing around the glider, a complete preflight inspection is in order.

DECISIONS

Improper preflight inspections are the cause of many glider accidents. Do not permit anyone to disrupt you while you perform this important inspection.

```
┌─────────────────────────┐
│  ┌───────────────────┐  │
│  │    CHAPTER 6      │  │
│  │                   │  │
│  │    CHECKLISTS     │  │
│  └───────────────────┘  │
└─────────────────────────┘
```

CHAPTER 6

CHECKLISTS

An experienced aerobatic pilot bails out of his crippled airplane, opens his parachute and falls to his death.

> Before takeoff, he failed to fasten the leg straps.

> The canopy opens at the beginning of a glider launch.

> The pilot loses control of the glider as he struggles to close it.

> A glider is seen very low in the landing pattern.

> The result of failing to properly set the altimeter before launch.

These and countless other accidents would not have occurred had the pilot used a simple checklist before the flight.

Ever wonder when the first aviator checklist was developed and used?

There is a fascinating article about checklists written by Atul Gawande, a medical doctor. One might think checklists are as old as aviation, but they are not. Serious interest in checklists dates back only to 1935, and was spurred by a fatal accident of the first Boeing Model 299 bomber, which went on to become the legendary B-17. Dr. Gawande mentions this briefly in his article, but before moving on to that let's consider the aviation history in more detail.

•   •   •   •   •   •

How the Pilot's Checklist Came About
by John Schamel
Instructor, FAA Academy

(Reprinted with permission)

October 30, 1935

Wright Field, Dayton, Ohio

The final phase of aircraft evaluations under U.S. Army specification 98-201 (July 18, 1934) was to begin. Three manufactures had submitted aircraft for testing. Martin submitted their Model 146, Douglas submitted the DB-1, and Boeing submitted their Model 299.

Boeing, a producer of fighters for U.S. Navy aircraft carriers, had little success in commercial airliners or bombers for the U.S. Army Air Corps.

Boeing's entry had swept all the evaluations, figuratively flying circles around the competition.

Many considered these final evaluations mere formalities. Talk was of an order for between 185 and 220 aircraft. Boeing executives were excited — a major sale would save the company.

At the controls of the Model 299 this day were two Army pilots. Major Ployer P. Hill (his first time flying the 299) sat in the left seat with Lieutenant Donald Putt (the primary Army pilot for the previous evaluation flights) as the co-pilot. With them were Leslie Tower (the Boeing Chief Test Pilot), C.W. Benton (a Boeing mechanic), and Henry Igo, a representative of Pratt and Whitney, the engine manufacturer.

The aircraft made a normal taxi and takeoff. It began a smooth climb, but then suddenly stalled. The aircraft turned on one wing and fell, bursting into flames upon impact. Putt, Benton, and Igo, although seriously burned, were able to stagger out of the wreckage to the arriving safety crews. Hill and Tower were trapped in the wreckage but were rescued by First Lieutenant Robert Giovannoli, who made two trips into the burning aircraft to rescue both men

Both men later died of their injuries. Lt. Giovannoli was awarded the Cheney Medal for his heroism that day, but he died in an aircraft accident before receiving it. The investigation found "Pilot Error" as the cause. Hill, unfamiliar with the aircraft, had neglected to release the elevator lock prior to take off. Once airborne, Tower evidently realized what was happening and tried to reach the lock handle, but it was too late.

It appeared that the Model 299 was dead. Some newspapers had dubbed it as "too much plane for one man to fly." Most of the aircraft contracts went to the runner-up, the Douglas DB-1. Some serious pleading and politicking by Air Corps officers gave Boeing a chance to keep the Model 299 project alive. Thirteen aircraft were ordered for "further testing." Douglas, however, received contracts for 133 aircraft for active squadron service. The DB-1 became the B-18.

Twelve of those Boeing aircraft were delivered to the 2nd Bombardment Group at Langley Field, Virginia, by August, 1937. The 2nd Group's operations were closely watched by Boeing, Congress, and the War Department.

Any further accidents or incidents with the Model 299 would end its career.

Commanders made this quite clear to all the crews. The pilots sat down and put their heads together. What was needed was some way of making sure that everything was done; that nothing was overlooked. What resulted was a pilot's checklist. Actually, four checklists were developed —

Takeoff, Flight, Before Landing, and After Landing. The Model 299 was not 'too much airplane for one man to fly', it was simply too complex for any one man's memory.

These checklists for the pilot and co-pilot made sure nothing was forgotten. With the checklists, careful planning, and rigorous training, the twelve aircraft managed to fly 1.8 million miles without a serious accident.

The U.S. Army accepted the Model 299, and eventually ordered 12,731 of the aircraft they numbered the B-17. The idea of the pilot's checklist caught on. Checklists were developed for other aircraft in the Air Corps inventory.

• • • • • •

How important are checklists? As it turns out, they are very important. Taking the time to use simple checklists in our daily flying routines proves to be a life and death decision.

Here is the web link to a fascinating article written by Dr. Atul Gawande — not about aviation checklists, but as used in medicine:

http://www.newyorker.com/reporting/2007/12/10/071210fa_fact_gawande

The essence of the article is this:

Because of infections, a simple checklist was proposed for doctors to use in a hospital Intensive Care Unit (ICU) for inserting ("setting") intravenous lines.

The checklist includes: a total of five simple steps starting with the obvious ones of washing hands and cleaning wounds.

Surprisingly, the use of the checklist was strongly resisted by doctors. But after one year, with the insistence and supervision of nurses, IV line infections fell from 11% to Zero!

At Johns Hopkins hospital, the average length of an ICU patient stay dropped by 50%.

Conclusion: the use of checklists for this one simple procedure prevented 43 infections, 8 deaths, and saved two million dollars — in a single hospital!

Reviewing recent glider accidents reveals several common, often repeated omissions to pilot responsibilities that are easily prevented by the use of simple checklists:

· Canopy Unlocked	· Flat Tire
· Dive Brakes Unlocked	· Knot in Tow Rope
· Tow Plane Running Out of Gas	· Seat Belts Undone
· Altimeter Set Wrong	· Pitot Cover On
· Tail Dolly Still On	· Control Locks On
· Controls Not Connected	· CG Out of Limits
· Flaps in Wrong Position	

Glider pilots are encouraged to use checklists. There are several common checklists.

1. Assembly checklist
2. Critical Assembly Check
3. Preflight checklist
4. Pre-takeoff checklist
5. Pre-landing checklist

As indicated by Dr. Gawande, using checklists saves lives, and are simple to use.

Glider pilots need to be educated on the simple process of using checklists, and should encourage fellow pilots to take the time to perform the checklist before and during each flight.

Not all checklists are created equal. It is common to see checklists omitting important items, or are poorly organized.

Your glider probably has a manufacturer's written checklist in view of the pilot. This checklist may or may not be adequate. Here is an example of the entire pre-launch check from a popular training glider's official flight manual:

"Before every takeoff check canopy and airbrakes for complete locking."

Here is another, far more complete checklist:

Wing and tailplane connections checked?
Full and free movement of controls?
Parachute secured?
Straps tight and locked?
Brakes closed and locked?
Trim correctly adjusted?
Altimeter adjusted?
Canopy locked?
Cable on correct hook?

The second one is much more complete, isn't it? You would likely make some additions to this list.

Nearly 20% of all fatal glider accidents occur during the launching phase of flight. Even more dramatic, is the fact that launching accidents usually occur during the first

20 seconds. Nearly all of these accidents would have been prevented with the simple use of checklists!

Each of us can help. We need to watch out for one-another. **Pay attention**. When you see someone assembling a glider without using a checklist, or failing to perform a critical assembly check, or hurrying through the pre-takeoff checklist, politely offer to help and suggest taking a few moments before the launch to ensure the glider is really prepared and safe for flight. It will have a big impact on glider safety. **It will save lives**.

In the hospital scenario, nurses interact with doctors and thereby help ensure the proper use of checklists. With this personal quality control method, hospitals and doctors are performing their duties to a higher standard, reducing accidents and preventing deaths.

The soaring community can use this model to good advantage to reduce glider accidents.

CHAPTER 7

PRE-TAKEOFF CHECKLIST

Before each takeoff, the pilot must be sure the glider is ready for flight. To do this in a systematic order, a checklist is used so nothing is overlooked. Many gliders have a written checklist posted in the cockpit. Others have none. It is common practice to use a memorized checklist whenever there is none posted. Even when a checklist is posted, it is a good idea to do both the written checklist and a memorized one, because the written checklist may not be complete. The written checklist may include unusual items pertaining to a particular aircraft only.

The following is a common written checklist:

Full and free movement of controls?
Ballast weights in place?
Parachute secured?
Straps tight and locked?
Pedals adjusted and locked?
Brakes closed and locked?
Trim correctly adjusted?
Altimeter adjusted?
Canopy locked?
Cable on correct hook?
Beware of crosswind!

A common memorized checklist is easily remembered with the letters CBS WIT CBE.

C	Controls	—	Check all controls for freedom of movement and proper takeoff position.
B	Ballast	—	Check for proper weight and balance and ballast is secure.
S	Straps	—	Seat belts secure and snug.
W	Wind	—	Direction and speed.
I	Instruments	—	Adjusted and proper reading.
T	Trim	—	Set for takeoff.
C	Canopy	—	Closed and locked.
B	Brakes	—	Dive brakes closed and locked.
E	Emergency	—	Emergency plan

Pilots who fly flapped sailplanes insert an **"F"** to form the word "SWIFT".

CB - SWIFT - CBE   It is probably not a good idea to insert the F if you are not flying a flapped sailplane because you may develop a habit of doing nothing when an item is checked.

When performing a checklist, actually touch and/or move the item as each item is announced aloud.

Many accidents have occurred simply because the pilot did not check one of the items. Do not permit others to rush you when you are preparing for launch. The chapter titled, "PT3" will include additional pre-takeoff thoughts.

As an instructor, I often notice pilots who use the manufacturer's checklist, which only mentions the altimeter, fail to check other important instruments before takeoff. Also, I notice many glider pilots who were trained in gliders with the less common ABC checklist actually fail to commit it to memory, so it can be recalled for gliders without a posted checklist.

In my case, I have added items I consider important and easily forgotten. "Remove wallet" is one of those items. Sitting on my wallet during a long flight can cause severe back pain. "Unzip fly" is another important preflight item, as it is difficult to accomplish during flight.

Computer systems are far more complex than the good-old-days. Without a checklist, it is easy to forget to enter crucial preflight information.

The checklist I use in my personal glider is a modestly lengthy one, and includes setting the flight computer, data logger, and other important items, any one of which might prevent a successful flight.

CHAPTER 8

AEROTOW

After finishing the cockpit checklist, have a qualified person connect the tow rope. Give the wing runner a thumbs-up signal when you are ready to proceed. The wing runner should look around to be sure traffic is clear, level the wings, give the 'take up slack' signal and, when the rope is taut, look at you and pattern traffic again, watch for your confirming rudder waggle signal, before giving the 'go' signal.

While this is happening, watch the tow rope to see knots don't form. (Knots reduce the strength of the tow rope up to 50%.) Watch the wing runner to see if they are looking for traffic. You are in an awkward situation since you can't see behind the glider.

The tow pilot is watching for both your rudder waggle and the wing man's go signal before beginning the launch. If the launch begins before you are ready, release immediately.

Many glider clubs and commercial operations modify this procedure. Be sure to follow your instructor's procedures.

At the beginning of the tow, hold the control stick in a position so when enough air is blowing across the wings, the glider will take off. This usually means the stick will be held about 1/4 inch aft of the neutral position. You are setting the elevator so the angle of attack of the wing is established, and all that is needed is enough airflow over the wings to generate enough lift to fly. Designers actually build aircraft this way. This system also works in Piper Cubs to C5A's. Some pilots make the mistake of moving the controls too much during the initial takeoff, thus creating pitch oscillation problems.

Keep the wings level with coarse movement of the ailerons. If there is a crosswind, the upwind wing should be kept slightly low. Steer the glider with the rudder until it is airborne. As the speed increases, the controls become more effective. Use the elevator to balance the glider on its main wheel, leaving the tail wheel or tail skid just off the ground. The glider will take off as soon as there is adequate lift. It is important not to keep the glider on the ground longer than necessary, nor force it off the ground too soon. In crosswind or gusty conditions, it is best to allow the airspeed to be slightly higher the moment of takeoff for better control.

The glider will normally take off before the tow plane. As the towplane accelerates and the speed increases, the glider will tend to fly higher. Hold it just a few feet off the ground with a slight forward stick pressure until the tow plane is airborne. If the glider pilot allows the glider to get too high on takeoff, the tow plane cannot take off and may even nose over. The tow pilot is quite justified in releasing the tow rope if the glider is ever too high.

The glider pilot must be prepared to release the tow rope at any time if things don't appear right. For this reason, the glider pilot should have his or her left hand ready to pull the release knob during the tow.

CROSSWIND TAKEOFFS

A crosswind can cause the glider to weathervane into the wind. In severe cases, the glider's rudder cannot prevent the glider from swerving into the wind. For this reason, the glider should be positioned on the downwind side of the runway to allow adequate room to stop the glider and prevent any collision with objects on the upwind side of the runway.

The wing runner should hold the upwind wing slightly low, and the pilot should hold slight aileron pressure into the wind in order to keep that wing low. The crosswind will try to weathervane the glider into the wind, so you will need to hold downwind rudder to prevent weathervaning.

During the ground roll, hold the upwind wing low to help prevent the wind from drifting the glider sideways. Use whatever rudder is necessary to control direction to follow the tow plane. A higher than normal takeoff speed is desirable to make a clean takeoff. This will help prevent the glider from settling back to the ground.

The glider will normally become airborne before the tow plane. The glider pilot must "crab" the glider sideways into the wind to offset the wind drift, and at the same time, maintain position directly behind the towplane.

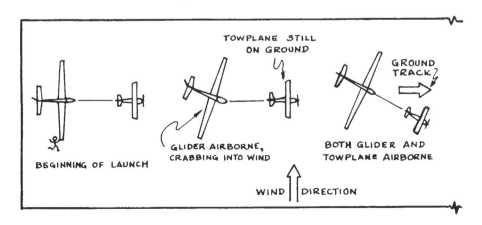

After the tow plane becomes airborne, both the tow plane and glider must crab sideways along the runway. It is important for the glider pilot to fly directly behind the tow plane in proper position once the tow plane is airborne.

ON TOW

Aerotow is one of the more difficult parts of the training program. Your instructor will allow you to do your best until things appear to be getting out of hand, and then take the controls long enough to put the glider back into proper position before giving them back to you. Most power pilots are able to do a satisfactory job after a few tows.

The correct tow position behind the tow plane looks like this:

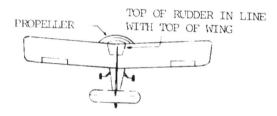

To be in the correct high tow position, the glider is positioned slightly above the towplane's prop wash. Your instructor will help you maneuver the glider down to feel the prop wash. Move the glider slightly higher, and note the "picture" you see of the towplane. One useful indicator to maintain this position is aligning the sailplane behind the towplane so the top of the tow plane's rudder is approximately lined up with the top of its wing. The glider is above the tow plane's prop wash. On some tow planes, the rudder will slightly protrude above the wing.

Another indicator is the "picture" of the towplane seen in the windshield of the glider. The towplane will be slightly above the glider's instrument panel.

Finally, the towplane will appear to be approximately on the horizon. Actually, the towplane may have its wheels or the wing above the horizon depending on the type of towplane, the type of glider being towed, and the speed.

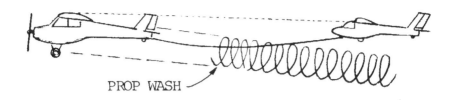

PROP WASH

If you begin to get too high, the towplane's rudder will appear to go down the wing.

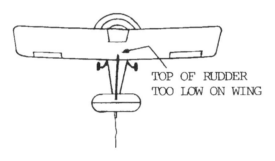

TOP OF RUDDER
TOO LOW ON WING

If you get too low, the rudder will stick up above the tow plane's wing and you may feel the turbulence of the towplane's wake.

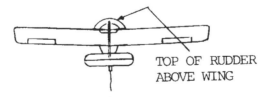

TOP OF RUDDER
ABOVE WING

When flying straight on aerotow, you will be straight behind the tow plane and you will be able to barely see both sides of the towplane's fuselage. If you drift to one side, you will be able to see only one side.

Keep the glider's wings parallel to the towplane's wings. During a turn, the glider's wings will be banked at the same angle as the towplane.

TURNS ON TOW

During a turn, fly the glider on the same arc as the towplane is flying.

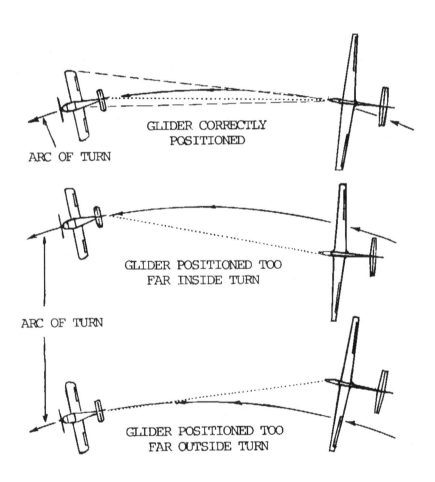

GLIDER CORRECTLY
POSITIONED

ARC OF TURN

GLIDER POSITIONED TOO
FAR INSIDE TURN

ARC OF TURN

GLIDER POSITIONED TOO
FAR OUTSIDE TURN

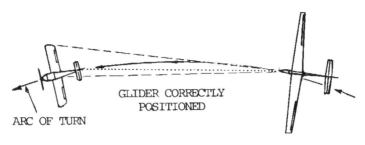

GLIDER CORRECTLY
POSITIONED

ARC OF TURN

When in the correct position, the glider will point towards the towplane's outside wing tip and you will be able to see only the side of the towplane's fuselage towards the inside of the turn. Both the towplane's and glider's wings will point to the center of the arc. You should still line up the top of the rudder with the top of the wing.

During aerotow, use coordinated controls to stay in the correct position. If you have the common problem of seesawing back and forth behind the towplane, it will almost always be because you are not using enough rudder to counteract the aileron drag.

The primary hazard during aerotow is getting too high above the tow plane. The glider can get high enough to lift the tail of the tow plane and cause a dive towards the ground.

> IF THE GLIDER GETS SO HIGH THE PILOT LOSES SIGHT OF THE TOWPLANE, THE PILOT MUST RELEASE AT ONCE!

NOTE: A possible exception is when an instructor is on board giving dual instruction. Releasing at a low altitude in a training situation may be hazardous. You should confer with the instructor as to how the instructor wants to handle this potential situation.

RELEASE FROM AEROTOW

At release altitude, look to the left and right to clear the area, then pull the release knob with your left hand. You will hear the release, but watch the tow rope to ensure that it is really disengaged before performing a level turn to the right.

Never do a climbing turn off of tow because of other situations where a climbing turn off of tow could be hazardous. For example, if you develop a habit of pulling the release and doing a climbing turn off tow and someday the release fails, you may pull the tail of the towplane up and to the side causing a diving turn opposite to the direction you are going. This could cause structural damage to the towplane or the glider. Your instructor will help you avoid developing dangerous habits.

SLACK ROPE

Slack in the tow rope can only occur if the glider has a faster speed than the towplane. This can happen should the towplane slow down suddenly, but this is not very likely.

The most common time to have slack in the rope is during, and especially after turns. If the glider pilot permits the glider to be incorrectly outside the circular arc of the path of the towplane, the glider is then on a larger arc. Since the glider is flying a greater distance, it will have to be flying a faster airspeed.

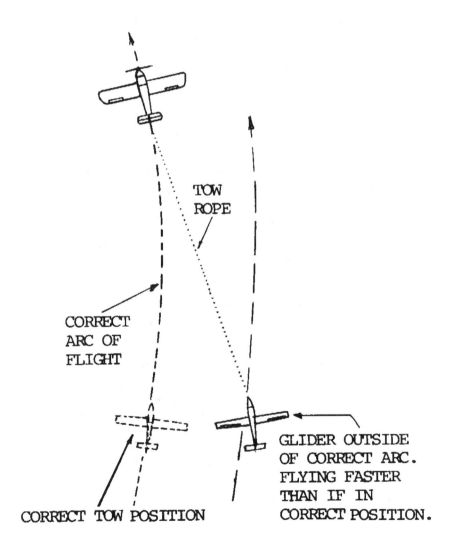

TOW ROPE

CORRECT ARC OF FLIGHT

CORRECT TOW POSITION

GLIDER OUTSIDE OF CORRECT ARC. FLYING FASTER THAN IF IN CORRECT POSITION.

The slack occurs when the glider moves back into the correct position because it is flying faster than the towplane. To prevent slack from forming, the pilot must gently move back into the correct position gently, with perhaps some small application of the dive brakes for increased drag.

Slack is most likely to occur when the glider is outside the radius of the turn and the towplane straightens out. This will leave the towplane and glider flying different speeds. The glider moves forward and slack forms.

It is also possible for the glider pilot to allow the glider to rise to an extremely high position during tow, and in attempting to get back down to the correct position, cause slack in the tow rope.

Extreme turbulence can also cause slack to form.

GETTING RID OF SLACK

Modern tow rope is very shock absorbing without being springy. For this reason it isn't likely you will encounter severe slack in the rope. Minor slack doesn't require any particular response.

Moderate slack should be removed by first doing nothing. The towplane will speed up slightly when slack forms because the towplane isn't pulling anything and the slack will be removed. Simply assume and hold the correct tow position.

If the rope is allowed to come tight with a hard jerk, the rope might break. To help soften the jerk, the glider pilot can yaw the glider away from the rope by applying rudder an instant before the rope comes tight. When it does come tight, the nose of the glider will be pulled around and thus soften the shock.

If you yaw too early or apply dive brakes while maintaining position, you might cause the glider to slow down. This causes a greater speed differential between the towplane and glider, which can cause the rope to break.

Another method to remove slack is to lower the nose of the glider just before the rope comes tight to accelerate the glider to the approximate speed of the towplane. This technique requires more skill.

If the slack is severe, it may be best to release the rope to prevent any possibility of the rope fouling on the glider.

RECOMMENDED STANDARD AMERICAN SOARING SIGNALS

Launching safety requires clear signals, predictable intentions, and plans for emergency action.

ON GROUND:

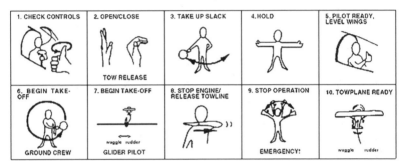

IN AIR:

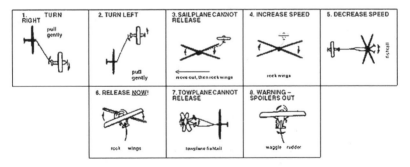

SOARING SOCIETY OF AMERICA, INC.
Avenue A & Jack Gomez Boulevard • P.O. Box E • Hobbs, New Mexico 88240

CHAPTER 9

SIGNALS ON AERO-TOW

There are standard signals which are used to signal the tow pilot to speed up, slow down, turn left and right, and the glider can not release.

When signaling, don't be too insistent, and don't expect immediate results. A tow pilot has a very difficult job and is used to glider pilots being out of position because of turbulence or lack of skill. When a glider pilot signals the tow pilot to turn, it isn't necessarily likely the tow pilot will be paying attention at that moment. It is also possible the tow pilot has a good reason not to turn in the direction requested (another aircraft in the area). If a glider pilot is overly demanding and moves to an extreme side position, the full power of the towplane's rudder can be overcome and cause the towplane to turn. It may also cause the towplane to begin a diving turn which the tow pilot may not be able to avoid. The resulting side load on the tow release mechanism can make it impossible for the tow pilot to release. The towplane and glider could crash together.

If you must signal, simply move out to position gradually and wait. Be patient. The tow pilot will get the idea eventually and begin a turn. You cannot demand the tow pilot turn; you can only request. The tow pilot may have a good reason not to turn.

On a turbulent day, the towplane's wings may rock, but this doesn't mean a signal to the glider pilot to release — or does it? This can be a tough one to decide, but this writer's opinion is if you are in turbulent air and the towplane's wings rock, stay on tow — don't immediately release until you get additional indications there is a problem.

If there is a serious problem, the tow pilot isn't required to go through the courtesy of giving a signal. The tow pilot may simply release the tow rope. The glider pilot should understand in a real emergency situation, neither pilot has any responsibility towards the other.

It unfortunately occurs that a glider pilot takes off with the dive brakes closed, but unlocked. (The pilot did not do an adequate pre-take off check, and line personnel failed to notice). As the tow proceeds, the suction on the top surface of the wing pulls open the dive brake and the towplane may not be able to continue climbing. The dive brakes typically open very slowly in this situation, and it is common for the glider pilot not to notice.

The signal for this occasion is for the tow pilot to waggle the towplane's rudder. Literally, the signal means "There is something wrong with your sailplane — check the dive brakes". This rudder waggle signal is also the "I cannot release either," signal the tow plane would use in the event both the glider and the tow plane couldn't release. Since this double release failure is unlikely and would only occur at high altitude after a specific sequence of events, the same signal can be used.

If you are ever on tow and the towplane is not climbing well — check the dive brakes.

Should you experience a release failure, it will almost always be a maintenance problem — something you should have noticed during the preflight inspection. The signal to use in case of this emergency is for the sailplane to be moved to the left side and rock its wings.

An important consideration of this signal is if you begin the signal by moving out to the right side, the tow pilot may think you have released and have begun to make a normal right turn after release. Since the tow pilot is expecting you to make a right turn after release, he or she may begin a descending left turn while you are still connected! So the signal the glider can't release is to move to the left and rock the glider's wings.

Do not move out to an extreme position. The tow pilot probably suspects a problem because the tow has proceeded above the usual release altitude. Remember you are only 200 feet apart. You can even use hand gestures. And last — if you both have a radio — call instead of signaling.

If you cannot release, the tow pilot is supposed to return to the airport and release you. After the towplane releases the tow rope, the rope may release from the glider with back pressure but without a radio you will not have any way to confirm this. Be sure to plan your pattern to assume a 200 foot rope is beneath you.

In the unlikely event neither the sailplane nor tow plane can release, you will have to land together. After the signals are given and you realize the towplane cannot release either, you should move to the low-tow position.

The reason for the low-tow position is to give the glider a buffer in case the towplane begins to descend too rapidly. The towplane can descend quicker than the glider, so the glider pilot should be prepared to open the dive brakes (almost always needed in this situation) and also side slip in order to match the tow plane's descent rate.

The tow pilot should come down very slowly with large, shallow turns, a wider than normal landing pattern and longer final leg. If possible, the people on the ground should be alerted to the emergency so the runway is well clear.

The towplane and glider will have to land together. A possible problem is a collision as they try to stop. A sharp tow pilot will stop the engine as the towplane touches down, to prevent the propeller from doing any damage.

The towplane should touch down just to the left of the centerline of the runway and the glider should touch down just to the right of centerline. The glider pilot should plan to pass the tow plane on the right side if necessary. (Both aircraft are turning the same as a normal release.) Most glider wheel brakes are inadequate at best, so be cautious in attempting to stop both the glider and towplane with the glider's wheel brake.

44

The tow pilot should coast to a stop with no brakes, staying in front of the sailplane as long as things are under control. The glider pilot should attempt to use the wheel brake enough to keep slack in the tow rope and avoid a collision.

One last word of caution — in case of a double release failure, you should not attempt to break the tow rope. You have never tried this before and the procedure is not suggested or described in any text book. Chances are the rope will not break. You will be jerked severely, perhaps causing structural damage and almost assuredly causing you to slingshot forward. Then you will have a huge, very dangerous slack rope problem.

CROSS-COUNTRY AERO-TOWS

If you ever make a long cross-country aero-tow, say 50 miles or more, try using a 300 to 400 foot tow rope. It makes it ever so much easier.

Every so often, you will have to make a takeoff without a wing runner — an unassisted takeoff. If this is necessary, you should use special precautionary procedures.

The glider pilot should position the glider on the downwind side of the runway with the upwind wing placed on the ground, and the glider placed at a slight angle to the direction of takeoff.

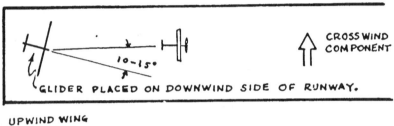

CROSS WIND COMPONENT

10-15°

GLIDER PLACED ON DOWNWIND SIDE OF RUNWAY.

UPWIND WING ON GROUND.

If the downwind wing is on the ground during the early takeoff run, the pilot will find it very difficult to bring the wings level. A ground loop may be caused by the downwind wing dragging the ground at the beginning of the takeoff. With the upwind wing on the ground at the beginning of the takeoff, in most cases the pilot will find it is easy to level the wings during the earliest moments of the tow.

Placing the glider at a slight angle will cause the trailing wing to swing forward as the towplane accelerates, helping to raise that wing.

A crosswind striking the glider's tail will cause the glider to weathervane into the wind, and possibly swerve or ground loop into the wind. This is why the glider is placed on the downwind side of the runway. It permits the most room in case the pilot cannot control the glider's ground track. Depending on wind strength, glider type, and strength of the tow plane, some swerving is to be expected. The pilot should be prepared to release in case the glider swerves severely.

All sailplane owners manuals address the problem of crosswind takeoffs. Each sailplane has a maximum crosswind takeoff capability. Most sailplanes cannot be launched if the crosswind is more than 15 m.p.h..

The glider pilot should not hook up the glider to the tow rope before getting into the glider. Gliders have been launched with no pilots in them! Since there is no one to run the wing, it is presumed only the glider pilot and tow pilot. After the glider pilot is seated in the sailplane with seat belts fastened and pre-takeoff checklist completed, the tow pilot can then connect the rope to the glider.

The tow pilot would then board the towplane, start the engine, and take up the slack. An agreed upon final "go" signal would be used to commence the tow. This can be a waggle of the sailplane's rudder but radio communication is preferred.

The glider pilot should hold the controls in a manner to pick up the wing that is on the ground (control stick towards the downwind side of the glider) and try to prevent the crosswind from pushing the tail downwind by deflecting the downwind rudder fully.

The controls won't respond immediately and the glider may begin to veer into the wind until the controls begin to become effective. The pilot must be prepared to abort the tow should there be any risk of loss of directional control. A pilot's unwillingness to abort the tow could cause a serious accident for both aircraft.

When the sailplane's controls do become effective, they often begin working suddenly. While holding fully deflected controls, the pilot must be prepared to quickly neutralize them so the glider doesn't over react.

CHAPTER 11

RUNNING THE WING

There will be times when you help someone launch their glider by running their wing. Do not hook up the tow rope to the glider until the pilot has completed the cockpit checklist. While waiting for the pilot to complete the cockpit checklist, be alert for other traffic and potential hazards such as people, parked gliders or other objects too close to the towplane/glider takeoff path. Carefully look at the entire length of the tow rope for knots which may have formed.

Show the end of the rope to the pilot so they can inspect the rope for condition. Carefully attach the tow ring to the glider release mechanism and give a jiggle to see and hear there is freedom of movement. If the ring is tight in the mechanism, it may be the wrong type of tow ring not installed properly, or there may be damage of the mechanism or rings.

After the tow rope is attached to the glider, give it a good strong tug, then walk to the wing tip of the glider. Stay well in front of the wing in case the tow plane pulls the glider forward. The wing could trip you, causing you to fall onto the wing, or injure you by striking your body.

On your way to the wing tip, **look at the canopy to see if it is locked, and also inspect the dive brakes to see if they are in the locked position**. If the glider is equipped with flaps, ensure they are in a logical position. These items are the responsibility of the pilot, but an alert wing runner can sometimes help prevent a pilot error which could cause an accident.

Wait for the glider pilot to give the signal to proceed with the launch, and then give the "take-up slack" signal. When the slack is removed from the tow rope, give the "stop" signal. Check once more for conflicting landing traffic, receive final confirmation that the pilot is ready to launch, and give the "go" signal to the tow pilot.

In most conditions, you need to support the wing tip for just a few strides before letting go of the wing tip. In any case, be sure not to grip the wing tip, or hold onto it too long. If you do, you may cause the glider to swerve or ground loop. Accidents have been caused by wing runners holding onto the wing too long. When running the wing, hold the trailing edge of the wing tip between two fingers. This will help to prevent you from holding on too tight.

Sometimes the pilot will hold inappropriate aileron pressure to one side while you are running the wing. You will feel pressure as the glider begins to move through the air. If you resist this pressure and then release the wing tip, the wing will suddenly tilt, perhaps contacting the ground and causing a ground loop. If you feel pressure while running the wing, it is better to allow the wing to begin to tilt while you are still holding it. The pilot will probably feel the wing tilting and remove the aileron pressure causing this undesirable action.

Nimbus 3 over Ridge Soaring Gliderport

CHAPTER 12

BOXING THE PROP WASH

During the glider pilot flight test, you will be asked to fly through and around the wake/prop wash of the towplane. This demonstrates your ability to control the sailplane in a smooth, coordinated manner, and shows your understanding of the position limits behind teh towplane and how to recover from an extreme tow position.

Instructors teach this maneuver in different ways, but what follows has become, more or less, the standardized technique.

Discuss with the tow pilot before the flight what you are going to do. It often inconvenient to have the discussion just before the flight. Most experienced tow pilots only need a simple, agreed upon signal from the wing runner indicating you are going to box the wash. The tow pilot will then expect the maneuver during the tow. One possible signal is to draw a square with your hands while the tow pilot is positioned to observe you. Be sure to receive confirmation from the tow pilot.

Sometimes you or your instructor will forget to have the tow pilot signaled before takeoff. If you attempt to box the prop wash by first moving to the side, a good tow pilot will take this lateral movement to mean you want to turn, for that is what you just signaled.

For this reason, the first step in boxing the prop wash should be to transition straight down through the prop wash to the low tow position. The tow pilot will feel this and expect you to maneuver around the wake.

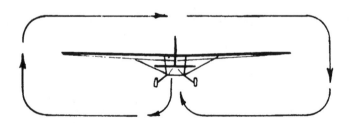

The examiner will be watching for smoothness in your flying, so you should attempt to move around the prop wash at a steady rate throughout the maneuver. The rate you are able to transition down through the prop wash without developing slack in the rope dictates the rate for the rest of the maneuver. A quick change of position is difficult, so don't try to maneuver too quickly.

At each corner of the box, you should briefly pause for one second.

The bottom position should be no lower than the standard low tow position. The low tow position is just below the tow plane's prop wash, which you will feel as you pass through it.

Once you are in the low tow position, you may move either right or left. The instructor will probably have you do it in both directions. To move laterally, you should initiate the maneuver with coordinated control motions — but gently. The glider will move to the side and you will have to stop the lateral motion by reducing the bank angle slightly.

You should move a limited distance to the side to prevent problems for the towplane. It is possible to overcome the rudder strength of the towplane and cause it to begin to yaw excessively. Use the tow plane's wheels as a guide as to how far out to the side to go. Line up the towplane's tail wheel with the opposite main wheel, or in case of a nose wheel towplane, line up the main wheel with the nose wheel.

As you climb up to the high tow position, you will have to hold just a little bank angle with the ailerons. Because the tow rope is pulling the nose of the glider sideward, you will also have to hold a little rudder to offset this. Both controls would be held to the outside of the box.

For safety reasons, it is never permissible to allow the glider to be above the normal high tow position. As you move up the outside of the box, be careful to not overshoot the high tow position. Line up the top of the tow plane's rudder with the top of its wing to judge how high to go. Going up is easier than going down while on tow. Since you are being tested, at least partially, on your ability to maintain a constant rate while boxing the prop wash, don't move too quickly.

Pause at the corner, and then move to the opposite side. Descending down to the low tow position is probably the hardest part of the maneuver. If you attempt to move down too quickly, you will produce unacceptable slack in the towline. Don't try to move too quickly.

Pause at the next corner, move back to the low tow position, and then move back up through the prop wash to the normal high tow position to end the maneuver.

CHAPTER 13

PREMATURE TERMINATION OF THE TOW (PT³)

During the aero tow, there are possible emergencies to consider. They are classified under the heading of "Premature Terminations of The Tow". They can include such emergencies as engine failure, running out of gas, or most common - rope breaks. It is important to realize these occasions **do** happen, even if they happen infrequently!

During one recent year, more than 30% of all glider accidents occurred during the first few seconds of the launch. There is really no excuse for not being prepared for this emergency. Before take off you should mentally prepare yourself for an emergency and have a plan of action. Your mind, and left hand should be ready to pull the release.

A premature termination of a tow is anything causing the aerotow to cease before the pilot intended. A rope break or other event occuring above 600 feet seldom causes any serious concern, but the same occurrence at low altitudes has resulted in many accidents. This chapter discusses some of the possibilities and suggests procedures a pilot can use in case a PT³ occurs.

A premature termination of a tow can occur in a variety of ways.

1. Rope Break
2. Canopy not latched
3. A control not connected
4. Wing drop (groundloop)
5. Air brakes opening
6. Flaps in wrong position
7. Towplane power failure
8. Tow speed to slow or fast
9. Being towed too far downwind
10. Controls hooked up backwards
11. Tire blow out
12. Tow rope will not release
13. Glider becomes too high
14. Someone moves onto runway
15. Tow rope catches on something at beginning of launch
16. Slack rope / rope wrapping around glider
17. Improperly installed component
18. PIO
19. Frozen controls
20. Turbulence
21. IMC
22. Inability to recover from low tow position
23. Knot in rope
24. Overrun tow rope
25. Traffic conflict / mid-air collision
26. Wing runner error
27. Airspeed indicator not working
28. Altimeter not adjusted properly
29. Tail chute opens
30. Water ballast disconnects and spills into cockpit
31. Snake / Bee / Wasp in cockpit
32. Unbalanced ballast in wings
33. Seat belts undone
34. Pitot / Static ports clogged
35. Smoke in cockpit
36. Panicky passenger.
36. Seat cushion / ballast bag moves
37. Controls restricted.
38. Tail Dolly On.
39 Canopy fogs up.
40. Others I haven't though of.

"Anything that can happen is going to happen <u>on this tow</u>" should be the last thought a glider pilot or the tow pilot should have as the tow begins.

After the early training flights, aero-tow becomes easier and the actual flying of the aircraft becomes more or less automatic. At this point, well before solo, as you begin each aero-tow, a great deal of your concentration should be given to what you will do when the rope breaks on tow.

The most critical period is during the first 600 feet of altitude or so. After you have gained 600 feet, you will have more time to react to an emergency and will have more options.

Pilots who have been trained for winch launching are better prepared for rope breaks. During a typical winch training course a student pilot will experience several cable breaks (real and simulated), and witness even more by other pilots. Things occur rapidly on a winch tow, and often when the glider is in an extreme nose high attitude. The glider pilot must be prepared to react instantly and correctly. Every winch pilot has a specific plan of action should the cable break at any time. So should pilots who launch by aero-tow..

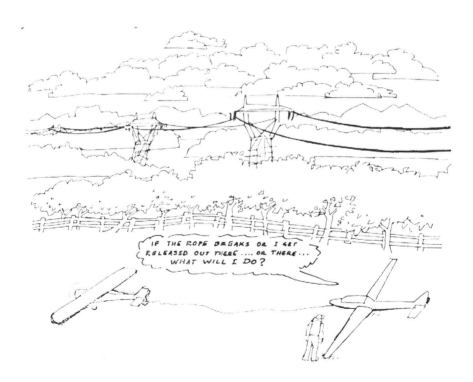

We should inspect the winch pilot's training and incorporate what we can into our own plan of action should our tow rope fail.

The winch pilot is READY. The left hand is on the release knob at the beginning of the tow and remains there until release.

Most instructors don't teach students to have their hand on the release knob during an aero-tow. (The student may release inadvertently). You must resolve this issue for yourself. You should at least have your left hand very near the release knob during the early stages of the aero-tow. However, having your hand on the release knob during a tow in heavy turbulence is probably not a good idea.

Very frequently, the rope breaks during the first part of the tow, well before the sailplane is airborne. This is when the strain on the rope is the greatest, not withstanding any jerks as the slack comes out during the tow.

The reason the rope breaks at this early stage is often because it is worn out, frayed, cut or perhaps because a knot has formed. A knot can reduce the strength of a rope by nearly 50%. It isn't practical to inspect every inch of the tow rope before each and every tow, but the glider pilot should inspect the rope near the tow ring where it is under the greatest strain and also watch the rope for knots as the tow plane pulls the slack out. Remember, the responsibility for preflighting the tow rope lies with the pilot in command of the glider.

If the rope should break at a very early stage, there isn't much to be concerned about. Simply roll to a stop. However, if you are moving along at 10 M.P.H. or perhaps just about to become airborne, you will have to keep calm and avoid running into anything or anyone. It's surprising how difficult it is to find the wheel brake under a high-stress situation when you are not prepared.

If you are airborne when the rope breaks, you may have to act quickly to prevent overrunning the end of the runway. The first step on any rope break while airborne will be to lower the nose to maintain flying speed. A stall from even five feet of altitude can cause significant damage. The second step is to get your hand on the dive brake handle in order to control where you will touch down and stop.

At this point we are assuming you are able to land and stop straight ahead on the runway. Now let's backtrack and suppose you did not have a rope break. Let's suppose instead that it was a partial or catastrophic engine failure in the towplane.

This puts a whole new light on the problem because now you must avoid colliding with the towplane which will be landing on the same runway, and is connected by a tow rope only 200 feet in front of you!

Under these circumstances the tow plane is *supposed* to release the tow rope, land on the left side of the runway and taxi off the left edge to avoid a collision. The glider is supposed to release the tow rope, land on the right side of the runway and taxi off the right edge of the runway. In this instance, both aircraft are turning the same as they would from a normal release from tow.

54

Suppose instead of an engine failure the tow pilot had a fire on board. As you can imagine, there isn't anything more terrifying for a power pilot than fire. Your tow pilot may panic. You might not be able to see the fire from the glider. What you will see happen is a sudden loss of power and the towplane descending back to the runway. The tow pilot may even jump out of the towplane before it comes to a complete stop. He or she might forget to shut off the engine and the towplane might ground loop and start coming towards your glider with that big propeller turning.

In these last two scenarios you can see the importance of the glider pilot being able to react quickly to the situation. In both cases the towplane pilot is under high stress and may not pull the release. (In many cases the tow plane release knob is in a dumb place.) The glider pilot must be prepared to release instantly in order to avoid a collision. (Tow pilots should be briefed for this emergency so they turn the engine off.)

The rule during the first few hundred feet of aero-tow should be that you, the glider pilot, have your hand on or near the release knob, ready to act in an emergency. If you have your hand on the knob, you should just rest your finger tips on it to avoid accidental release.

Now on to the next phase. You find yourself too high to land and stop straight ahead on the runway, but too low to perform a 180 degree turn back to the runway. In this case you will have to land somewhere else. Where you go should have been determined before you took off. One of the serious mistakes pilots make before they fly at a new site is not asking the local pilots what they would do when a rope break occurs.

There are a number of possible ways to handle this emergency. You might be able to land on a different runway (turns up to 90 degrees may be possible, but be very careful not to try this too low). More likely you will have to land in one of the available farmer's fields beyond the end of the runway. Maybe there is no place to make a safe landing and you will have to crash into trees or whatever. The important point is to ask for advice from local pilots **before** flying at a strange site.

Several points come to mind in case of a rope break:

1. Be sure to lower the nose of the glider to maintain flying speed.

2. Release remaining tow rope only if you have time. This is usually not extremely important.

3. You may turn either right or left. This is an emergency and not a normal tow release.

4. Minor turns can be made regardless of altitude. In general, your limit should be no more than 90 degrees in direction (not bank angle) if you are below 200 feet. But don't continue a turn so long you catch a wing tip on the ground.

The most serious mistake is to attempt a 180 degree turn back to the runway at an insufficient altitude.

If you are too low to complete the 180 degree turn, you will most likely stall and spin or strike the ground with a wing tip, causing the glider to cartwheel. In either case it is almost impossible to avoid serious injury.

Normally, the minimum altitude from which a glider pilot can safely accomplish a 180 degree turn is 200 feet. This minimum altitude would have to be raised to take into consideration aircraft performance, pilot abilities, wind, turbulence, and density altitude. For instance, 200 feet is quite safe for a Schweizer 2-33 near sea level but a heavy, slow rolling sailplane in the high mountains might not be able to do a safe 180 degree turn below 300 or 400 feet.

Everyone's instinctive reaction is to attempt the 180 degree turn and return to the field. It takes a strong, disciplined, well trained pilot to react properly to this emergency. No matter how much you read, no matter how much you are told, you are not likely to react properly unless you fully understand the problem, have a plan of action, and overcome your instinctive reactions in order to do the best thing.

It is far better to spend a few hours retrieving a sailplane from a farmer's field than to take months getting a sailplane repaired. Do not take any unnecessary chances. Even if you are above 200 feet, it still might be better for you to land in that giant farm field requiring no risk than to attempt a low turn you have never practiced.

The magic 200 foot minimum height is nearly universally accepted by textbooks and instructors around the world. If you experimented by first trying a 180 degree turn at 200 feet and then lowering this minimum turnaround altitude on subsequent test flights, you would find that a 180 degree turn can be made at lower altitudes in these test conditions. The 200 foot minimum altitude takes into consideration the element of surprise, the subsequent slow reaction time, and perhaps not totally perfect flying finesse by a pilot who is not as sharp as we sometimes misguide ourselves into believing we are. The firm rule is NEVER ATTEMPT A 180 DEGREE RETURN TO THE FIELD BELOW 200 FEET. Decide BEFORE you take off if conditions call for a higher limit.

How do you know you are above 200 feet? The only reliable way is to monitor the altimeter during this stage of the aero-tow. The altimeter has an unavoidable lag error, but this error benefits the glider pilot because the glider will be at least as high as or higher than the altimeter indicates.

Get into the habit of making note of the critical altimeter reading before each takeoff. Say to yourself, "OK, my altimeter is set at the field elevation of 1,250 feet. That means my critical altitude in case of a rope break is 1,450 feet." You now know what your responses will be. Below 1450 feet you will land straight ahead. Above 1,450 feet you know you can turn around because you are more than 200 feet above the ground.

Here's another important habit to develop: As you pass through 200 feet, or your predetermined decision altitude, <u>announce it out loud</u>! "200 FEET" or perhaps "Decision Point". If the rope breaks and you haven't announced 200 feet out loud, you know what your response will be. Land ahead! If you have announced 200 feet out loud and conditions are normal, you know you can perform a safe 180 degree turn.

No student is permitted to solo in our school unless the student reliably announces out loud "200 feet" on every flight. Any solo student who fails to announce the 200 foot mark on subsequent training flights or check rides, automatically receives a simulated rope break. Every student, including transition pilots, receives at least three rope break simulations before solo — one straight ahead rope break at the maximum altitude which still permits a straight ahead landing on the runway, and two 200 foot rope breaks.

Being able to make a safe 180 back to the field from 200 feet doesn't always mean you should. If you are above 200 feet and the rope breaks, your decision whether to turn back to the field is based on several factors:

1. Pilot currency. How sharp are your piloting skills?

2. Available emergency fields. Is a big, no-risk field ahead of you?

3. Distance from the airport. Perhaps you are at 200 feet but too far from the airport to make it back. The towplane will not to climb as rapidly on a hot, humid day would as it would on a cooler day.

4. Wind. Perhaps the subsequent tail wind is too strong for a safe downwind landing.

5. Towplane performance. Sometimes you gain so much altitude so fast, you might not be able to land and stop on the runway if you did turn around, especially when taking off into a strong wind.

THE 180 DEGREE TURN

Refer to the next chart. Notice the minimum altitude loss vs. angle of bank indicates the optimum angle of bank is 45 degrees. You lose less altitude performing a 45 degree banked turn.

Angle of bank degrees	Sink Speed knots	Rate knots	Load factor	Radius of turn feet	Time for 180° seconds	Altitude lost in 180° turn
60	64	3.92	2.0	208	6.1	40 ft.
50	56	2.69	1.6	236	7.8	36
45	54	2.34	1.4	255	8.8	35
40	52	2.07	1.3	281	10.2	36
35	50	1.87	1.2	315	11.8	37
30	48	1.72	1.2	361	13.9	40
25	47	1.61	1.1	427	16.8	46
20	47	1.52	1.1	528	21.1	54
15	46	1.46	1.0	698	28.2	70
10	46	1.42	1.0	1040	42.5	102
0	45	1.39	1.0	-	-	-

There are other reasons to use a well banked turn. The prime cause of a stall and spin during any turn close to the ground is the over use of the rudder in a subconscious attempt to make the aircraft turn quicker, coupled with the incorrect but instinctive attempt to hold the aircraft up with excessive back stick pressure.

The best and safest turn close to the ground is a 45 degree angle of bank. Of course you must be more than 1/2 wing span above the ground and consider wind gradient or turbulence. Regardless of the angle of bank you use, you must maintain a safe speed and keep the yaw string straight. The glider cannot stall or spin if you obey this rule. (More about stalls in another chapter.)

If the rope breaks, your decision as to what to do should be automatic. If you have announced "200 feet" you may turn around. If you have decided to perform a 180 degree turn, you must primarily pay attention to the airspeed and the yaw string. Executing the proper angle of bank becomes automatic with practice.

WHICH WAY TO TURN

If you decide to turn back to the field, you should normally turn into the wind. The wind will help keep you lined up with the runway and give you a shorter ground distance to travel. However, you may also have additional considerations such as avoiding obstructions by turning away from hills, trees, buildings, etc. Before takeoff, think about which way you'll turn if the rope breaks.

AIRSPEED

The airspeed you use cannot be too slow (you might stall), nor too fast. You cannot waste precious altitude with excessive speed. The speed to use during this 180 degree turn should be normal pattern speed plus an arbitrary 5 knots because it is an emergency. (Sometimes called the "wife and kids factor".)

Once the turn is accomplished, you will generally have a tail wind. You must maintain flying speed. Your ground speed will be much faster than normal, giving an illusion of a faster airspeed and possibly causing you to try to slow down and stall. Glance at the airspeed indicator more frequently than during a normal into-the-wind landing.

Drop the remaining tow rope only if it is convenient. Land, and then stop in a big open area. Remember the last 100 feet or so of the landing roll with a tail wind may be without directional control. Never attempt to taxi into a crowded area when landing downwind.

In summation, there are several key points to watch for during every flight and especially during simulated rope breaks:

1. Just before takeoff, are you thinking what you will do in case of an emergency, or the rope breaks? Which way will you turn? Is 200 feet the right minimum altitude for a 180 degree turn on this flight?

2. During the aero-tow are your fingertips on or near the release knob?

3. Do you always announce "200 feet" or "Decision Point" out loud? (Or a higher altitude, if appropriate.)

4. On simulated rope breaks, do you first lower the nose of the glider to maintain airspeed?

5. During any turn close to the ground, do you maintain a steady, correct airspeed, and keep the yaw string <u>absolutely</u> straight?

HOW THE TOW PILOT CAN HELP

One last point is the path the tow plane follows on takeoffs. It is normal to fly along the center line of the runway. In case of a rope break the glider pilot will need to make an additional turn at low level which can be very dangerous . . .

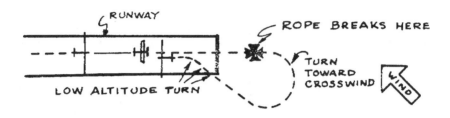

If the tow pilot would simply drift slightly downwind during the first 200 to 400 feet of climb, it would make a rope break safer for the glider pilot by eliminating that additional turn.

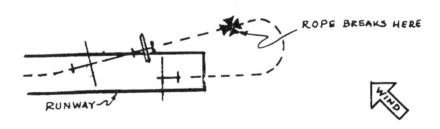

Schempp-Hirth Ventus 2

CHAPTER 14

LANDINGS

When entering the landing pattern, the glider must always be a little too high. Excess altitude is then bled off using the dive brakes as glide path control. It is a mistake to attempt to enter the downwind leg without using the dive brakes. It's not possible to be sure what kind of air mass you will be flying through as the glider approaches the landing pattern, so you must always be a little high and dissipate the excess altitude as you approach and fly the pattern.

Because you are in a glider without an engine, you will have to be prepared to modify the pattern in case the glider begins to lose altitude more quickly than anticipated.

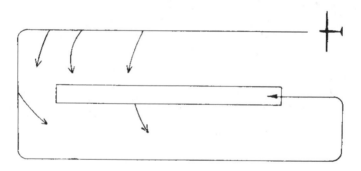

A glider landing pattern is essentially the same as a power plane pattern with one important exception — glider pilots don't do touch and goes!

Glider landing patterns are usually started slightly lower than the normal power plane pattern so the glider is approximately at 500 feet AGL opposite the intended touchdown point on the downwind leg. (Explanation to follow). This altitude should be raised in higher winds, turbulent conditions, or to match the power traffic pattern at power airports.

Airspeed is very important. Maintain a constant airspeed around the pattern. The pattern airspeed is usually the maximum L/D speed plus 1/2 of any wind, and more airspeed in turbulent conditions (The wife and kids factor.)

At the beginning of the landing pattern, perform the pre-landing checklist. This can be a written checklist, but most pilots use a standard acronym: USTAL.

U — Undercarriage (wheel down and locked.)
S — Speed established.
T — Trim set.
A — Airbrakes, place your hand on the handle and test them.
L — Look for other traffic, at the landing area, and at the wind sock.

During the down wind leg, be aware of the sink rate. If the glider is sinking rapidly, you may have to turn onto the base leg early. If the sink rate is not as fast as normal, you may have to open the dive brakes or extend the down wind leg further than normal. A normal sink rate during the down wind leg is 200 to 400 feet per minute (2 to 4 knots).

During the turn onto base leg, your primary attention should be on the yaw string (you   mu st keep it straight) and the pitch attitude so you don't permit the airspeed to fluctuate. At the same time, you need to look at the touchdown point to see if the glider will be in the "landing cone".

If it appears you are high, open the dive brakes and if necessary, turn slightly to extend the down wind leg a bit farther. On the other hand, if the angle looks shallow and looks like you are going to be low, you will close the dive brakes and abbreviate the base leg by turning onto final early.

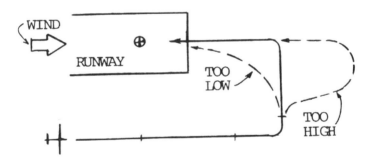

Glider pilots learn a technique to judge the landing pattern using easily identifiable angles. This technique is called TLAR, or "That Looks About Right." This angle judging system is superior to other systems using altitudes at certain key points in the landing pattern.

The problem with using specified landing pattern altitudes comes into play when flying cross-country and you need to land in some farmer's field. It is unlikely you will know what altitude the farmer's field is above sea level. There are sections of the country so flat a pilot might set the altimeter on 0, and fly a hundred miles with only minor terrain height variations. (The farmers fields are usually much bigger too.) However, a pilot who relies on the altimeter is at a severe handicap when flying in undulating terrain. Consider the following scenario:

If you took off from a gliderport with your altimeter set at 0, you might normally enter the downwind leg at an indicated 600 feet. When flying cross-country and forced to land out, you may enter the base leg at an *indicated* altitude of 600 feet, but you may not take into account the farmer's field is 200 feet higher than the takeoff point. This means you are only 400 feet above the ground on the downwind leg. The field may be very large, but you are under a lot of stress becasue this is one of your first off-field landings. Turning onto base leg at your customary 300 feet indicated, you realize that some mistake was made because the field appears very low on the canopy. You are indeed too low and land in an apple tree just short of the farmer's field. Using the TLAR angle system and appreciating the effect of wind on the glide ratio over the ground can help you avoid the problem.

The majority of off-field landing accidents tend to be overshooting accidents. Pilots invariably misjudge their pattern altitude and end up too high to get down and stopped in the remaining space. You can verify this statistic yourself at your home gliderport. Watch where the pilots land vs. where they intend to land. Most often, pilots who err will land beyond their intended touchdown point.

Many of the very serious accidents involve pilots who find themselves too high on their final approach. What do they do when they find themselves over the end of the runway (or farmer's field) at a height so excessive they can't land straight ahead, but are too low to do a 360 degree turn? There really isn't a good answer to this problem. What glider pilots typically do is one of two things:

One is to push the nose down and dive at the field or secondly, attempt a 360 degree turn even though they have been made aware of the hazards.

In the first case, the pilot ends up crashing into whatever is at the end of the field at a high rate of speed, or else the glider is forced onto the ground at high speed resulting in a series of crunching, porpoising bounces along the ground.

The second case is even more serious. When a pilot attempts to perform a 360 degree turn at a low altitude, they subject themselves to mistakes inherent to the most common of all fatal aircraft accidents. The pilot will instinctively resist turning at the steep bank angle necessary to complete the turn in the space available. Steep turns close to the ground are frightening and it is only natural for a person to resist them.

Since the pilot is reluctant to perform the required steep turn, they will unconsciously try to force the glider to turn quicker with the rudder. Pressing on the rudder, causes the glider to do a skidding turn. This skidding turn causes the glider to want to bank steeper and our hapless (hopeless?) pilot will resist by applying opposite aileron. In this skidding fashion the sink rate increases and the glider begins to descend more rapidly. The pilot will now make the final mistake by attempting to hold the glider up with increased back stick pressure. The glider stalls and spins at an altitude too low for recovery.

If you attempt a 360 degree turn at too low an altitude and fly the glider properly so it does not stall and spin, you may still catch a wing tip on the ground or crops. The glider could cartwheel across the earth. This will certainly cause severe structural damage and perhaps injuries to the pilot, but the chance of survival is better than spinning into the earth.

You can avoid these terrible accidents by simply learning the maximum capabilities of your glider and flying the pattern within acceptable limitations.

The glider has a maximum possible glide ratio. To avoid being too low in the pattern, divide this maximum glide ratio in two and never allow yourself to be below this glide ratio on final approach. The glider also has a maximum steepest possible glide ratio (The dive brakes open, wheel down glide ratio.) You should learn what this glide angle looks like and never be any higher than this on final. This usually means for a glider with a glide ratio of say 30 to 1, you should be in a 'cone' while on final approach between 15 and 5 to 1.

We judge heights in a number of ways:

1. Relative sizes of familiar things. (As we gain height things appear smaller.)

2. Depth perception. (Because our eyes are some distance apart.)

3. Angles.

If we are above 500 feet or so, our guesses using depth perception and relative sizes of things may be off by 30% or more. You can try this for yourself. With an instructor aboard, cover one of the altimeters in a two-seater, take a tow to an unknown altitude, then fly around for awhile and try to judge when you are at, say, 1,200 feet. You may get lucky, but the majority of the time you will be off by a significant amount.

I remember the first time I flew over the desert. Being from the eastern part of the United States, I was at a handicap because there wasn't anything I was familiar with to help me judge height. (How tall is a Yucca?) As a result, my first landings were more difficult.

While you are learning to land, you are making numerous identical landing patterns. The instructor is giving you a chance to develop judgment by giving you an opportunity to make many identical landing patterns, and also make mistakes while supervising your progress.

Students consciously or subconsciously learn if they enter the pattern at the same place and altitude, fly the pattern exactly the same way with turns onto base and final over the farm house at such and such altitude, the pattern will work out just fine. Well it will, especially on the calm days a student is normally learning to fly. But if the day is not calm, or if a landing has to be done where there is not a farm house, the student can be in trouble. The student has learned visual clues that will only work at one place, in one set of circumstances.

Angles don't lie. If you can learn what the steepest and the shallowest glide angles look like, you can then use the dive brakes and/or flaps to control the pattern and final glide within that cone for perfect control.

You can get a good idea what these angles look like by simply pacing off distances to simulate glide angles. Two of your strides are equal to about one of your heights. To simulate a 5 to 1 glide ratio, simply pace off 10 strides and look back to your starting point. The angle you are looking at is 5 to 1. To simulate a 15 to 1 glide ratio, pace off 30 strides. Take this book outside with a couple of markers, and actually do the above exercise.

The 5 to 1 glide ratio is the more important of the two. You must learn to judge this angle. As you fly the landing pattern, be sure to fly far enough on the down wind leg so you will be below this angle when you turn onto final.

It is obviously important not to allow yourself to fly so far along the downwind leg that you become dangerously low. Stay high within the landing cone. Remember the effect of wind on the glider's performance. On very windy days, you may have to turn onto the base leg not far from the downwind edge of the runway.

Another thing to watch for at your home airport is how people consistently turn onto base leg a little too soon. During off-field landings, pilots will do the same thing — only worse. Watch your own flying. If you notice you seem to be using full dive brakes during most of the final approach, you are probably guilty of this faulty flying technique. Except for practicing, side-slips during an approach are an admission of an improperly planned landing pattern. Pilots who is using full dive brakes or side-slips frequently should review their technique. They are most likely developing a habit of turning onto base too soon and too high.

Slips must be learned for the occasion when you have more altitude than you can loose with your dive brakes and/or flaps alone. Slips are especially valuable when crossing over obstructions bordering fields. They can become a habit however, and you should avoid situations where you must use a side slip to get down.

FINAL APPROACH

During the final approach, keep the airspeed constant unless there is a reason to change the airspeed such as unexpected turbulence or wind shear. Control where you will touch down with the dive brakes. After only a few landings, you will be able to judge the angles properly.

Very steep approaches, like any maximum performance maneuver, are more difficult to perform than shallower ones.

THE TOUCHDOWN

A normal touchdown should be a low-energy touchdown, which means at a minimum speed. This is to prepare you for off-field landings, when slow airspeeds on touchdowns will result in shorter roll-outs and less chance of damaging the glider.

A normal glider touchdown will be on the main wheel and tail wheel or tail skid at the same time. If you touch the tail wheel or tail skid slightly first, that's OK. In high winds, cross winds, and turbulent conditions, it is proper to land slightly faster for better control.

FAULTY APPROACHES

The instructor will give you opportunities to make mistakes and see how you respond to unusual and awkward situations. The faulty approach is one of the most important situations that can arise. This is a situation where you are at an awkward position to the landing area and must "make up" a safe landing pattern on the spur of the moment.

These kind of faulty approaches usually happen because you are trying your best to find lift and stay up instead of accepting the fact you should be in a landing pattern. You might bump into a thermal as you are turning onto the base leg. As you turn and turn in the thermal, you drift further and further from the field and then you have to make a long, straight-in approach. Worse yet, you find you cannot stay up, you are too far from the original field and must now select another field. From your new position, you may be entirely too low to perform a normal pattern.

Another common error is to make a long glide through heavy sink to a downwind leg. You may find yourself several hundred feet too low as you begin the pattern. You might also be on the opposite side of the landing area you are used to. Or you may find yourself mistakenly flying a pattern that would lead to a downwind landing, and then try to reverse your path to facilitate a proper into-the-wind landing.

It is not possible to cover every conceivable circumstance but several points come to mind:

1. At 1000 feet you should always be upwind of your landing pattern. You may still attempt to thermal, but while you are watching for lift you should be flying towards the crucial downwind leg.

2. Set your own personal minimum thermalling altitude limits. If you are a beginning pilot, you might set your own personal minimum altitude limit as 1000 feet. When you get down to 1000 feet you will ignore all lift and concentrate on the landing. As you gain experience you may lower your personal limit, but as a safe pilot you should still be conservative.

3. Always use a pre-landing checklist. This not only helps to check for important pre-landing items, but helps to organize your thinking and prepare your mind to switch to the 'landing mode'.

4. Never attempt to "stretch" a landing pattern. When you enter the pattern low, there is a great temptation to try to fly slowly and hold the aircraft up by pulling back on the stick. You continue on the downwind leg as though you are going to try to fly the same ground path as usual, even though you are too low to do so. That's because you really <u>are</u> too low!

5. Maintain a constant, proper airspeed and a straight yaw string. If you are a little low and notice the airspeed is below normal, you can bet it is because you are unconsciously pulling back on the stick in a futile attempt to hold the aircraft up. Low and slow is dangerous!

Refer to the next drawing: You are at point 'A' at 600 feet. There is a fairly strong wind. What should you plan to do?

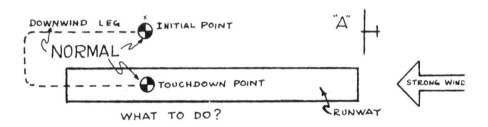

You cannot be at two places at once, so it won't be possible to be at the normal 600 foot point (x in the drawing above). You are going to be well below the proper altitude if you continue to the initial point. The wind is blowing hard enough you are concerned about turning around to make a down wind landing from a right hand pattern.

Answer: You have probably elected to continue on downwind, but turn onto base leg at about the midpoint of the field and land well along the runway as in the following drawing.

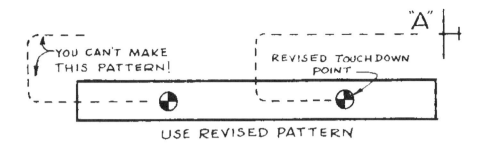

YOU CAN'T MAKE
THIS PATTERN!

"A"

REVISED TOUCHDOWN
POINT

USE REVISED PATTERN

On paper it's easy. In the real world there will be a great amount of pressure to try to fly the "normal" pattern. There are people on the ground watching and we don't like it when we are criticized by landing in other than the normal place. We would prefer no one noticed our low pattern entry error.

Mistakes are made by everyone. It is a part of being human. As a low time glider pilot, you will make your share of minor errors. Let's hope you don't try to cover up a minor error and as a result, commit a major error.

How about the following problem? You were trying to thermal a fair distance from the airport and run into severe sink instead. You start back towards the airport and find yourself at 800 feet at point 'A'. The normal left hand pattern is indicated. What would you do? There is no appreciable wind.

There are a couple of answers that come to mind. Let's assume you will be unable to make it to the normal pattern entry point (x). Did you think of the possibility you might still be able to perform a right hand pattern? Simply fly along the south side of the runway until you are at the pattern entry point on the opposite side of the runway.

If you encountered too much sink on the way to a right hand pattern, you could abbreviate the pattern and land well down the runway as in the previous problem.

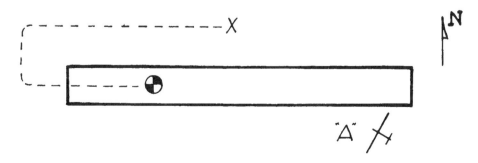

X

N

"A"

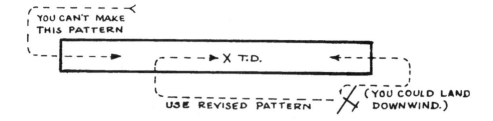

It might happen that a downwind landing is the safest thing to do. This last problem could easily be answered with a planned left hand or even a right hand pattern to a downwind landing. What if the pilot would have been at 500 feet at point 'A'? Or 300 feet? It's a good idea to run through some of these "what if" scenarios, especially with a group of other pilots, and compare answers.

Turns close to the ground are dangerous. We say this time and time again. One of the principle reasons for this extreme hazard is the psychological makeup each one of us possesses. You must realize the limitations each one of us has in high-stress situations. It is extremely important for you to develop good flying habits. Be prepared — have a plan of action — and most of all fly a safe, steady airspeed and _keep the yaw string straight_. In day-to-day flying, practice making well coordinated turns at a constant airspeed. Insist on precision in your flying, and with this discipline you will be a safer pilot.

CROSSWIND APPROACH AND LANDING

It often occurs you must land with the wind blowing across the runway. The same basic principles apply to the crosswind landing as a normal landing. Only the additional techniques required for correcting for wind drift need to be considered. (Also see the chapter on slips.)

Crosswind landings are more difficult than crosswind takeoffs because it is more difficult to maintain directional control while the speed is decreasing rather than increasing as during takeoffs.

There are two methods of handling the crosswind approach and landing, the crab method and the wing-low or slip method. The crab method is the easiest method during the approach phase of the landing, but it requires a high degree of judgment and timing to remove the crab immediately before touchdown. The wing-low, side slip method is recommended in most situations, but you may find it is often desirable to use a combination of the two methods.

The crab method is established by assuming a heading into the wind with the wings level so the glider's ground track remains aligned with the centerline of the runway. The yaw string would remain streamlined. The crab angle would be held until just prior to touchdown, when the glider must be quickly aligned with the runway using the rudder to avoid any sideward contact with the runway. A pilot may also use the crab method until just before round out and then smoothly change over to the wing-low method for the touchdown. Changing technique during the round out phase requires more pilot skill.

The wing-low method also compensates for wind drift. It also enables the pilot to maintain the longitudinal axis of the glider in line with the ground track and centerline of the runway throughout the final leg, round out, flare, and touchdown. This prevents any possibility of touching down sideways which can cause a dangerous ground loop or produce damaging side loads on the landing gear.

To use the wing-low method, simply align the glider's heading with the centerline of the runway, note the direction and amount of drift, and then apply drift correction by side slipping into the wind by lowering the upwind wing. The amount the wing needs to be lowered depends on the strength of the wind. When the wing is lowered, the glider will tend to turn in that direction. It is necessary to simultaneously apply sufficient opposite rudder to prevent the turn, and keep the glider's longitudinal axis aligned with the runway. The drift is being controlled with aileron, and the heading with the rudder. The glider is now side slipping just enough to offset the drift.

If the glider begins to move off of the centerline of the runway, it is an easy matter to either increase the bank angle, or decrease the rudder to realign things.

In a very strong crosswind, the glider's rudder may not be powerful enough to permit a severe slip. In this case a combination of the wing-low and crab methods will be necessary.

A glider has a maximum crosswind landing capability. Generally it is not possible to control the landing roll-out in direct crosswinds of more than 15 knots. If there is a strong crosswind you should use a different runway or possibly, if the landing area is large enough, land diagonally across the runway, thus lessening the crosswind component. (During final apprach, align the glider on the downwind side of the runway.)

CROSSWIND ROUND OUT (FLARE)

Generally, the round out will be made as in a normal landing. But you will have to continue holding crosswind correction to prevent drifting. As the airspeed decreases, the flight controls become less effective, so you may have to gradually increase the deflection of the rudder and ailerons to maintain the proper drift correction.

CROSSWIND TOUCHDOWN

At the point of touchdown, do not level the wings. Keep the upwind wing low throughout the flare and touchdown. If you level the wings, the glider will begin to drift, causing side loads on the undercarriage and a possible ground loop. CAUTION: It is possible to touch the upwind wing on the ground and cause a severe ground loop . If you are flying a low-wing glider or are flying in a strong crosswind, be careful not to have the wing so low that it touches the ground.

If you have been using the crab method of drift correction, the crab will have to be removed with the rudder immediately before touchdown to prevent side loads on the undercarriage. This requires precise timing and judgment.

If you have been using the wing-low method, the wing should remain low throughout the flare and touchdown. Gliders have a particular advantage over power planes in this respect because the pilot of a power plane is unable to keep the wings tilted until the plane stops. The power plane will eventually settle on all three wheels despite the efforts of the pilot.

After touchdown, be very alert to any tendency for the glider to swing out of control. Don't relax, and don't attempt to taxi near other aircraft or people. During the last few yards of the roll out, you will have very little control of the glider. As the glider's rudder loses effectiveness, the glider will tend to weathervane into the wind.

Keep the upwind wing low during the roll out, and ideally the upwind wing should come to rest on the ground as the glider stops.

If it is gusty or the winds are strong, it will be much more difficult to perform a landing in crosswind conditions.

GUSTY WINDS

To maintain good control in strong, gusty winds, use a slightly increased airspeed. If the glider has flaps, use only partial, or no flaps at all. This will permit the glider to land at a higher airspeed, and a higher nose-up attitude on final approach. This will require less of a pitch change during the flare and permit a higher airspeed to ensure better control during roll out. Be careful not to use such a high speed you can't get the glider stopped, and end up floating right past the intended touchdown point.

The normal pattern speed for windy conditions is to use the recommended no-wind landing speed and add one half the wind speed. If the air is gusty as well as windy, you might add a few knots for the wife and kids — but don't get carried away and use too much speed.

WIND GRADIENT

Wind gradient is a change of wind speed with altitude. It is caused by the surface friction of the air with crops, trees, buildings, and hills. A steep wind gradient is when the change in wind speed with altitude is very rapid.

Wind gradient affects a glider during both takeoffs and landings, although the landing phase is usually more serious. During the takeoff, a noticeable, sudden increase in airspeed will occur as the glider is towed through the wind gradient. This can be especially hazardous on a winch or auto tow when a sudden increase in airspeed can cause a cable break, cause structural damage to the glider, or even stall the winch engine. During an aerotow, a steep wind gradient will also cause a momentary increase in airspeed. However, the tow pilot should have been briefed on how to compensate for this, and not make any sudden control corrections to counter the surge in airspeed.

The following drawing shows an example of wind gradient. The most pronounced gradient will often occur just above ground level, up to about 200 feet.

Normally, wind has no effect on a glider's airspeed. In this case, however, the glider has considerable inertia. A sudden drop in wind speed, as in a steep wind gradient, causes a drop in the glider's airspeed as well. The wind speed drops very rapidly in a wind gradient and the glider finds itself changing quickly from flying against a strong head wind to flying against a much lighter one. A steep wind gradient could cause a stall if the glider entered it at a slow airspeed.

When flying through a suspected wind gradient, you should fly with extra airspeed. In severe cases an airspeed of 70 knots or more may be required for safety. Since a high wind speed means a low ground speed, high pattern airspeed does not mean landing far along the field.

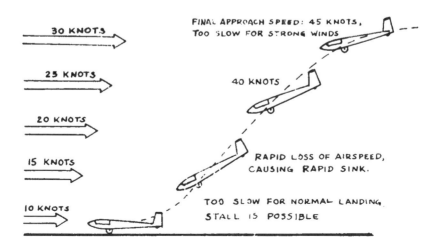

If there is a suspected wind gradient, it is important to avoid turns at low altitudes. Turns in a wind gradient will leave one wing flying in slower moving air than the other, which can cause the lower wing to loose lift or stall and cause an accident.

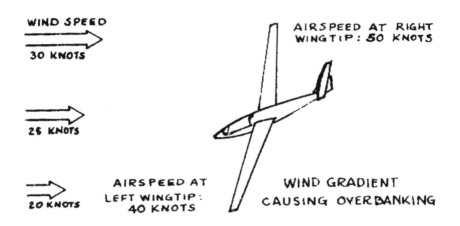

In windy conditions, plan the landing pattern to fly higher than normal. Maintain more altitude (steeper angle) while flying the down wind and base legs.

When turning onto final approach, be well above the wind gradient, and then descend through the wind gradient in a straight and level attitude, at a higher than normal airspeed.

The glider will tend to lose altitude rapidly as it passes through a wind gradient. Unfortunately, you may unconsciously pull back on the control stick in an attempt to arrest the descent, causing a risk of a stall. Be prepared to press the control stick forward at the first sign of diminishing airspeed in order to maintain airspeed.

The correct action when flying through a suspected wind gradient is to plan a higher pattern, and fly through the wind gradient in a straight and level manner at an airspeed well above normal. Anticipate the effects of the wind gradient and provide enough airspeed and altitude.

Once the glider is through the wind gradient, it will have extra airspeed to control gusts near the ground. You will have to avoid ballooning during gusts near the ground. If you do balloon, the glider will loose airspeed rapidly and a hard landing may occur.

HOW FAST IS THE WIND BLOWING?

A wind sock or a flag blowing straight out indicates a wind of about 20 knots or more. If the wind sock is out at a 45 degree angle, it is blowing about 10 knots. If the wind sock is blown over, it is blowing very hard!

74

CHAPTER 15

STEEP TURNS

It is surprising to learn continuous steep turns are often the most difficult maneuver to perform during the FAA flight test. Power pilots who are transitioning into gliders find this maneuver particularly difficult. The reason is because it is seldom a power pilot would make continuous turns. In fact, most turns in a power plane are either 90 degrees or 180 degrees.

Turns are supposed to be precise. Coordination should be perfect, and airspeed control should be accurate. The most common faults are incorrect use of the rudder during entry into a turn, slipping or skidding during the turn, excessive speed and/or the inability to maintain a steady speed, and not being able to recover on a specific heading.

To practice steep turns (40 - 45 degree angle of bank or more), you should begin by practicing coordinated entry into and out of turns. Perform several roll-ins followed by roll-outs of a turn. Are you able to keep the yaw string centered? The more quickly you move the ailerons, the more difficult the coordination is with the rudder. Start by gently rolling into the turn and gradually build up to a more brisk turn entry.

As a glider is banked into a turn, the nose wants to drop. If you don't resist it, the airspeed will naturally want to increase. To avoid this happening, note the pitch attitude with the horizon before you roll into the turn. As you roll into the turn, pay particular attention to the position of the nose in relation to the horizon. Maintain the same pitch attitude by increasing back pressure on the control stick as the bank angle increases. With practice, you should be able to maintain a constant airspeed and a straight yaw string as you roll in and out of a steeply banked turn.

Note: As you roll into a turn, the nose of the aircraft does not drop instantly. There is a delay before back stick pressure is required. The next time you fly, try making some turn entries without using back stick pressure, and notice when the nose begins to drop.

Watch the horizon, while circling, not the airspeed indicator. By watching the horizon you will be able to notice any pitch attitude changes causing the airspeed to change. You will also have the benefit of seeing the yaw string at the same time, so you can adjust for any minor yaw corrections. All of this will make you fly more precisely, and simultaneously provide you with yet another important benefit.

While watching the horizon and the yaw string, you will also be watching outside for other aircraft. This will make you a safer pilot as wellas making you a better soaring pilot because you will begin to notice other sailplanes, dust devils, cumulus clouds, etc. for signs of lift. Expert glider pilots spend most of their time looking outside the glider for indications of lift. Beginners spend too much time looking inside the glider at the instrument panel.

What speed should you fly during a steep turn? About the only time you do continuous turns is while thermalling (or taking flight tests). While thermalling, fly the best speed for minimum sink at the angle of bank you are using. Many factors enter into the formulation of the exact best speed to fly in this circumstance. Fortunately, the performance curve is reasonably flat at minimum sinking speeds, so there is a wide speed range available for use without being penalized.

We may know the listed minimum sinking speed for a particular glider is, say 40 knots. This is the minimum sinking speed for straight gliding flight. In a turn, the minimum sinking speed will increase because centrifugal force causes an increase in weight. (Wing loading increases). You can simply add another 5 knots to the speed and be reasonably close to the optimum speed for bank angles up to about 30 degrees.

Steeper angles of bank will require even higher airspeeds. If the glider is carrying water ballast, the extra load will require another 5 knots of airspeed. If it is a turbulent thermal, you may need to add a few knots to maintain control. Some sailplanes seem to climb better at what might be considered too fast an airspeed.

For steeper angles of bank, the airspeed must either be increased before the bank angle increases or be allowed to increase as the bank becomes steeper (preferred). As the desired bank angle is reached, considerable back pressure will have to be applied to provide the necessary angle of attack for the increased load.

The outer wing is flying a greater distance than the inner wing during turns, and therefore has a greater airflow over it, which creates greater lift than the inner wing. This unequal amount of lift creates an "overbanking tendency" which must be overcome to prevent the glider from increasing its bank angle. To counteract this overbanking tendency, hold steady opposite aileron pressure during steep turns.

For the flight test you will be expected to select an appropriate airspeed for the bank angle and be able to maintain a steady airspeed during the turns, while maintaining coordinated flight and watching for other aircraft. Being able to stop turning on a prescribed heading or towards some object on the horizon is simply a matter of practice. Begin the recovery 10 degrees or so before coming to the desired heading.

CHAPTER 16

FLIGHT AT CRITICALLY SLOW SPEEDS (INCIPIENT STALLS)

During the flight test, you will be asked to fly the glider at a speed just above stall. The examiner will be watching if you understand the problems of slow speeds and high angles of attack and how to properly use the controls.

"High angles of attack" are the key words. At very slow speeds, you are flying very close to the critical angle of attack. Any increase of the angle of attack will cause a stall to occur with resulting loss of lift. In addition, any increase in weight or wing loading will also cause a stall. (Wing loading is the amount of weight per square foot the wing is supporting.)

During critically slow airspeeds, the controls are not very effective and any course, overuse of any of the controls may cause a stall. The control stick will be held well back to maintain the high angle of attack necessary for the slow speed. Be careful not to move the stick back any further. One useful hint is to use the horizon as an attitude indicator to maintain a steady pitch attitude, and thus a steady airspeed angle of attack. Only glance at the airspeed indicator from time to time to verify you are flying at the selected airspeed.

During flight at a critically slow speed, if a gust causes a wing to begin to bank (glider to roll) while trying to hold a straight glide, it may not be possible to roll the wings level by using opposite aileron without stalling a wing.

Remember, ailerons work by changing angle of attack. Picking up a falling wing with ailerons, you will be increasing the angle of attack of a wing that may be already at, or near, its critical angle of attack and that wing will stall.

As you build flying hours you will develop certain habits. Many habit patterns become nearly instinctive. One of these instinctive reactions will cause you to attempt to pick up a dropping wing with opposite aileron, and coordinated application of rudder. More than 99 per cent of the time this will be the correct reaction. But, during flight at critically slow airspeeds, reacting in the usual manner, may cause one wing to stall. This can result in a spin.

When flying at very high angles of attack, develop skills and perceptions that make you think, and fly differently than while flying at higher speeds. Your mind has to 'shift gears' to keep from making mistakes.

To correct for a dropping wing during a flight at a critically slow airspeed, you must use opposite rudder. Let's suppose the left wing is going down. At critically slow airspeeds when one wing drops, you must assume it is stalled. There are actually two problems . . . first, one wing isn't producing enough lift (the left one in our example) and second, the other wing is producing too much lift.

Attempting to use the ailerons will only aggravate the situation. Opposite aileron usage will lower the left aileron in our example, causing an increased angle of attack on the portion of the wing already at, or near, its critical angle of attack.

However, opposite rudder, (right rudder) will cause the glider to yaw, swinging the stalled wing forward, increasing its relative airspeed and decreasing its angle of attack so it becomes unstalled, producing more lift and raising the wing. The right wing in our example is still producing lift — too much lift — and is slowed down when opposite rudder is used, so it produces less lift which lowers that wing.

So, at critically slow airspeeds, keep the wings level and correct for a dropping wing by using opposite rudder.

During the flight test you will be asked to perform turns while flying at a critically slow airspeed. Remember, an aircraft gains weight due to centrifugal force in a turn, so the wing loading increases. During critically slow airspeeds you must use very gentle bank angles. To make a quicker rate of turn requiring a steeper angle of bank, you will have to increase the airspeed.

The uninformed person believes the rudder turns an aircraft. As a matter of fact, all of us at one time thought the rudder turns the aircraft. We have nearly an instinctive intuition about mechanical things which helps us figure out how things work.

Unfortunately, we are not always correct. This is especially true of our mistaken belief that a rudder turns an aircraft.

This misconception of the rudder causes most pilots to use excessive rudder during turns. It has been said the majority of all fatal aircraft accidents are the result of the pilot using excessive rudder in the direction of the turn. Doing this while at a critically slow airspeed can cause the lowered wing to slow down beyond the critical airspeed and stall. Thus, the incorrect reactions of a pilot must be suppressed and new reactions developed by thorough training and practice.

How much rudder is enough? How much is too much? These questions are easily answered. While making any turn. . . use as much rudder as necessary to keep the yaw string straight. As amazing as it may seem, we could eliminate one of the major causes of all fatal aircraft accidents by simply keeping the yaw string straight with judicious use of the rudder. This is especially true during flights at critically slow airspeeds and during any turns close to the ground such as: the landing pattern, low altitude thermalling and low altitude emergencies such as rope breaks.

During the flight test, the examiner will watch closely how you react should a wing begin to bank while at critically slow speeds. Don't use opposite aileron — use opposite rudder.

The examiner will also watch how you make all other turns. Be careful not to use excessive rudder. Keep the yaw string straight!

Finally, you will be watched how you control the airspeed. Don't stare at the airspeed indicator. Watch the horizon and hold a constant pitch attitude (relative position of the nose below the horizon) to maintain a steady speed.

CHAPTER 17

FORWARD STALLS

A stall occurs when the wing (airfoil) reaches its critical angle of attack.

Stalls are really dangerous. When a stall occurs, the aircraft wing looses a great deal of its lift, and the aircraft descends rapidly. How much it descends depends on several factors, but it can be hundreds of feet.

When an aircraft stalls, the pilot may panic, and when the pilot panics, he or she probably won't react properly. Remember that first rope break? How did you react? Probably you didn't react altogether correctly. Anytime we do something for the first time we are likely to be flustered and not react in an entirely reasonable fashion. Remember the first time you had to react to an emergency while driving a car?

Human beings don't always react predictably to high stress situations. Instructors try to overcome this by giving you the opportunity to undergo potentially dangerous experiences while you are with an experienced flight instructor who can guide you through acceptable reactions.

Most of the stalls you practice will be the kind people normally experience in the real world; gentle, insidious, slowly developing. The kind you might cause accidentally when distracted.

Another aircraft in the pattern, a child on the runway, an off-field landing, these and other distractions can easily divert your attention away from flying the glider correctly. Once your attention is focused on another matter, your subconscious mind has the opportunity to "take over". Your subconscious will cause you to pull back on the stick to keep the aircraft from going down, and to press on the rudder in an attempt to make the glider turn, or turn quicker.

You don't think so? Well, just remember these words. I guarantee your instructor or some other instructor in the future will point out these improper reactions — and it will probably be during a high-stress situation.

These incipient, slowly developing stalls are what you need to practice the most, for they are the most likely to cause you serious problems. While practicing them, try to simulate what we have just described: begin at about 50 knots or, better yet, your normal landing pattern speed. Set the trim for this speed as you normally would during a landing pattern. Gently ease back on the stick and slowly — ever so slowly — increase the angle of attack until a stall occurs. Note the six signs of an impending stall as they occur. Learn them in this order. Say them out loud:

```
┌─────────────────────────────────────┐
│                                       │
│   1. Excessive back stick pressure.   │
│                                       │
│   2. Nose high attitude.              │
│                                       │
│   3. Low airspeed.                    │
│                                       │
│   4. Quietness.                       │
│                                       │
│   5. Mushy controls.                  │
│                                       │
│   6. Buffeting.                       │
│                                       │
└─────────────────────────────────────┘
```

Then, as the stall occurs — at the first buffeting — make a recovery. How did you do? If the wing started to bank, did you attempt to correct with opposite rudder? Or did you allow your subconscious to cause you to incorrectly use the ailerons in an attempt to pick up the wing?

On the stall recovery, move the stick forward to force the nose of the sailplane below the horizon. Don't move the controls too abruptly, and don't overdo the recovery so you force the nose severely below the horizon resulting in excessive airspeed and loss of altitude.

Learn to notice an impending stall as soon as you notice any one of the six signs, and then make a corrective control movement before the stall occurs.

This next statement will get me into trouble with strict theorists. If you simply keep the glider's nose below the horizon at all times, it is highly unlikely you will ever stall. Possible exceptions include flying in extreme turbulence, wind shear, and extremely aggressive overuse of the controls. Develop the habit of checking the pitch attitude, especially during any low altitude turns, and keeping the nose of the glider below the horizon. Don't over do this, or you could then develop another bad habit by flying too fast.

Theory states it is possible to stall a glider in any pitch attitude or airspeed, including when the nose is pointed straight down. This is because a stall is a function of angle of attack and not pitch attitude. However, aircraft designers are restricted by design limits so they can not make the elevator too powerful. The result is simple:Assuming the type certificated glider is within weight and balance limitations, it is not possible to stall the glider if the pilot simply keeps the nose below the horizon in a normal glide attitude. A little experimentation while accompanied by an instructor will demonstrate these facts.

While flying at a normal speed with the nose below the horizon, it is impossible to increase the angle of attack without raising the nose of the glider. the pilot would fly a faster speed in severe turbulence, which precludes the possibility of stalling.

CAUTION: Abrupt control deflections above maneuvering speed can damage the glider.

By the way, have you wondered what causes the aircraft to buffet as it approaches a stall? It is caused by the resulting turbulent air from the wing striking the tail, causing a shaking of the whole glider. Sometimes the turbulent airflow on top of the wing will also produce skin vibrations and noise noticeable in the cockpit, especially in metal gliders.

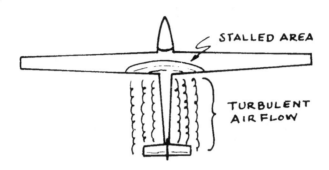

THE SAFETY CHAIN

You might discover an idea others have thought of to prevent stalls. Why not install a chain from the control stick forward to some structural part of the glider, so the pilot could not pull the stick back far enough to stall? The amazing thing is that this would work! For a couple of dollars in material, the glider would be unstallable. In fact, aircraft have been built with a simple control stop that restricts elevator movement so the pilot cannot pull the control stick back far enough to stall the aircraft.

However, a word of caution. The problem with this '"safety chain" is we would find it difficult, if not impossible to slow the glider down enough to make a landing. We would be forced to contact the ground at an excessive, dangerous speed. Takeoffs could also be equally impaired.

Stalls can be caused by excessive use of the rudder and/or when the angle of attack is near the stall. We would have to restrict the aileron and rudder usage with a similar "safety chain". In fact, such an aircraft with severely limited controls has been built, and for a large percentage of flying, we would have sufficient control.

But with these restricted controls, normal takeoffs and landings would be very difficult and we would not be able to fly at all even in light turbulence. Modern aircraft designers give you enough control movement to allow controlled flight in normal conditions, but they try not to give you excessive control effectiveness.

The best place for your "safety chain" is in your mind. We don't have a fool proof, practical aircraft, but we can certainly try to have a fool proof, practical pilot.

DEEP STALLS & REDUCED G'S

There are rare occasions when a glider can be stalled in a very nose high attitude. Incorrectly performed aerobatic maneuvers come immediately to mind. Another more unexpected time might be during the climb stage of a winch or automobile tow. These types of ground launches require the sailplane to climb quite steeply. If the towing cable should break and the pilot does not react properly, then a stall can occur with the nose pointed well above the horizon.

Some people enjoy these deep stalls, but most of us are bothered by the feeling of one's stomach moving up to our throats. A few people are totally incapacitated by the negative 'G' sensations of the stall and may "freeze" on the control stick or react in some other inappropriate manner.

It is important to be fully aware of the six signs of an impending stall. It is hoped with thorough training and practice you will react to any one of these signs and make a recovery before a stall actually occurs.

It is equally important to understand the sensation of one's stomach-up-in-the-throat is not necessarily a sign of a stall. This uncomfortable feeling is caused by a reduction in 'G' loads during many maneuvers, or by flying in turbulent air.

We are normally experiencing one 'G' or one gravity. A person will weigh nothing in a zero 'G' condition such as the astronauts experience.

While flying straight and level, if you move the stick forward, you will feel yourself becoming lighter. You are experiencing a reduced 'G' sensation. You have felt the same sensation while driving a car over a sharp rise in the road.

During most stall recoveries, you will feel this reduced 'G' sensation, but you must understand this feeling by itself does not mean you are stalled. If you are especially sensitive to the reduced 'G's, you will probably need more training than other persons. It is possible for some people to be so severely affected that they would be unable to qualify for a pilot's license. But this is rare.

If you don't like stalls, that is normal. Most people don't. However, you must become proficient at stall recognition and stall recovery to obtain a license and be a safe pilot, so let's get on with it.

During deep stall practice, the nose of the glider will be brought well above the horizon. The speed will dissipate rapidly. When the stall occurs, the wing will be more deeply stalled than during a gentle stall, and the nose will drop sharply.

When the deep stall occurs, the nose of the glider will fall well below the horizon regardless of what the pilot does. Even if you hold the control stick fully back, the nose will still drop, and will go well below the horizon.

With the nose pitched down below the horizon, the speed will build quickly and the wing will unstall. Then the nose can be brought back up to a normal flying attitude by applying the correct back pressure on the control stick.

The object of practicing deep stalls is for you to make a prompt, positive recovery with a minimum loss of altitude. As noted, the glider will recover from the stall even if you do the wrong thing and hold the stick all the way back. If you continue to hold the stick back, the glider would then continue to do a series of deep stalls and recoveries.

Your job is to help the glider recover with a minimum loss of altitude. At the point of the stall, simply move the stick slightly forward of the neutral position, allow the nose to drop below the horizon, pause long enough for the airspeed to recover, and then — when the wing is unstalled and flying again — ease back on the stick to bring the nose back up to a point below the horizon where a steady, stable gliding speed can be maintained. (Read this paragraph again.)

CAUTION: If you abruptly move the stick forward to begin the recovery, you might produce negative 'G's which would make dirt and other loose objects fly up in the cockpit. They could get into your eyes, blinding you. Better to secure all loose objects and keep the interior of the glider clean.

When the nose is well down and the glider is in a reduced G state, if you abruptly move the stick back you could cause a secondary stall. In addition, if you were flying above maneuvering speed, structural damage could occur.

SECONDARY STALLS

The problem with any secondary stall is not one of aerodynamics but of psychology. If an accidental stall occurs, it will usually happen when you are least expecting it. This element of surprise may cause you to panic or at least put you under great stress. If you don't make a positive recovery on the first attempt, and a secondary stall occurs, you have a very real chance of panicking and you may not be able to react in a rational manner. It is important to be proficient at stall recognition and recoveries. Beware of the accidental secondary stall.

Schleicher ASK-13

CHAPTER 18

TURNING STALLS

If a glider stalls during a turn, the inside, or down wing, will tend to stall first. That's because the inside wing is traveling a shorter distance and therefore is flying at a slower airspeed and a higher angle of attack than the outside wing.

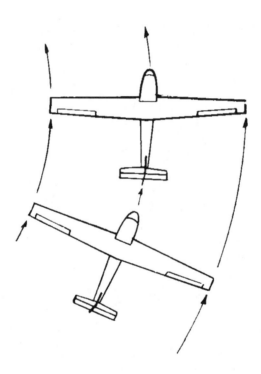

Just as in a forward stall, the turning stall occurs because the wing is at an excessive angle of attack. However, unlike the forward stall, there is an additional problem caused by the unbalanced lift forces causing the glider to roll toward the down or stalled wing. Simply reducing the angle of attack by moving the stick forward does not stop this imbalance and rolling motion. We can't use the aileron to stop the rolling motion because putting the stalled, inside wing's aileron down, only aggravates the stalled situation by increasing the angle of attack of the stalled wing.

The first step to recover from a turning stall is to push on the opposite rudder.

Opposite rudder will yaw the glider, swinging the stalled wing forward, which increases the airflow on that wing and helps that wing become unstalled. Opposite rudder also slows down the unstalled wing so that wing produces less lift. This helps make the whole wing produce a more balanced force and stops the rolling motion.

The second step to recover from a turning stall is to move the stick forward to reduce the angle of attack of the entire wing.

Step three is very important. After the first two steps, we must give the glider time to recover from the stall. The third step is to pause so adequate flying speed is regained.

After the pause, and only then, may the ailerons be used to roll the glider level.

The step-by-step recovery procedure for a turning stall is:

---

1. **Opposite rudder.** } (may be done simultaneously.)

2. **Stick forward.**

3. **Pause, regain flying speed. (Very important.)**

4. **Roll level with ailerons and coordinated rudder, then bring nose to normal gliding attitude below the horizon.**

The first two steps can be combined into one, but you must think and say the steps in the above order. You'll see that spin recoveries are done in the same order.

During the initial practice of turning stalls, it is important to use only shallow to moderate bank angles. These are the most common conditions encountered by pilots when they have accidents. The glider will want to increase its bank angle as the stall is approached. Care should be taken to continue a steady rate of turn until the stall occurs by keeping the wings banked at the same angle throughout the maneuver.

Recoveries should be prompt, with a minimum loss of altitude by using the controls in the proper sequence. It is perfectly acceptable to combine steps 1 and 2 — opposite rudder, stick forward, as the first step. However, there must then be a pause to allow the wing to become unstalled before any opposite aileron is applied. The instructor will be especially alert for any premature aileron usage during the recovery.

At the moment of the buffet, you will probably be holding a slight opposite aileron pressure. This will slow the recovery process, so you must remove this offending opposite aileron pressure by bringing the stick to a neutral position.

Turning stalls should be practiced both with dive brakes and/or flaps deployed and retracted. That's because a turning stall could occur in the landing pattern when these devices are being used.

Inadvertent turning stalls are most likely to happen during turns close to the ground. Rope breaks and the 180 degree turn back to the airport, low altitude thermalling, and turns in the landing pattern are prime culprits to the safety record. By one estimate, fully three fourths of all fatal aircraft accidents can be traced to the turning stall at low altitudes.

It is very important to understand it is extremely difficult, if not impossible, to stall a glider in turns of 30 degrees angle of bank or more.

The reason is because the elevator is designed to have a limited effect. In a steep turn, nearly all, if not all of the elevator's authority is utilized to produce the extra lift needed in the turn. Your instructor will demonstrate this fact by having you enter a turn with a bank angle of more than 30 degrees and then having you attempt to stall the glider. Without an abrupt, violent motion of the controls, you will find it impossible to stall the glider.

In steeper turns, as the airspeed dissipates, the lift the wing's are producing becomes insufficient to hold the glider up, and it begins to slide down sideways through the air, long before a stall can occur. This sideways motion of the relative airflow causes the nose to yaw sideways.

When practicing turning stalls, watch the nose of the glider. If the nose only yaws through the horizon, you haven't stalled at all, and the controls still work in their normal fashion. If the glider truly stalls, the nose will pitch down through the horizon, or if only one wing stalls, there will be an obvious rolling motion.

THE DIFFERENCE BETWEEN STALLING AND FALLING

The difference between stalling and falling is in the one case, the controls continue to work in a normal fashion, and so the pilots natural, instinctive reactions will be correct. In the other, instinctive reactions will be incorrect and the situation can become much worse. In both cases altitude is lost.

It's an amazing fact that from the standpoint of stalls, steep turns are safer than shallow ones. During training, you will practice making gentle banked turning stalls. You will see that even the docile trainer is much easier to stall and reacts more violently in this configuration.

WARNING: During windy conditions, or days with strong thermal activity, there is often severe turbulence, wind shear, or a high wind gradient at altitudes from ground level to several hundred feet. It can be very dangerous to be turning in this turbulent zone. The need for steep turns close to the ground should be avoided, especially in windy or turbulent conditions.

To prevent turning stalls, learn to make well coordinated turns at a constant, proper airspeed. **Keep the nose of the glider below the horizon and the yaw string straight!**

Duo Discus over Seminole Lake Gliderport

CHAPTER 19

CROSSED-CONTROL STALLS

The objective of this maneuver is to emphasize the importance of flying the sailplane properly — using coordinated controls and proper airspeed whenever performing any turn. This exercise will help you understand what happens if a pilot allows his or her instinctive reactions to "take over" in a high-stress, poorly planned turn. Especially when the glider is close to the ground.

The crossed control type of stall occurs with the controls "crossed" — aileron stick pressure in one direction while the rudder is held in the opposite direction. Let's look at a typical scenario and see how a pilot might allow instinctive, incorrect reactions overcome proper training:

Accidents occurring as the result of a crossed-control stall are most frequent during five occasions:

      1. Low landing pattern entry.

      2. Low altitude thermalling.

      3. Low altitude rope break.

      4. Poorly planned and executed base to final approach.

      5. Overshooting the centerline of the runway, followed by a button hook pattern.

All of these incidents have two things in common: Low altitude turns and high stress.

Our hapless pilot misjudges the pattern entry and is lower than intended on downwind leg. Instinctive behavior will cause the pilot to make two mistakes at this point: The pilot is likely to fly too close to the runway, and may incorrectly attempt to hold the glider up with the misconceived "up and down" control by holding back on the control stick.

Since the pilot is flying the downwind leg too close to the runway, there is not enough room for a proper base leg and the pilot will have to make a steep 180 degree left turn in order to line up with the centerline of the runway.

(See drawing on next page)

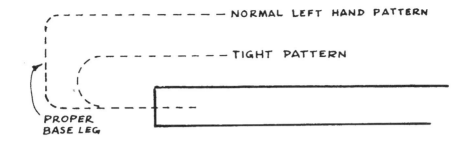

Instinctive behavior will cause the pilot to pull back on the control stick in a futile attempt to hold the aircraft up, or to reduce the rate of descent. The pilot's attention may be directed outside at some distraction such as another glider taking off the landing runway. Often, an inordinate amount of time is spent looking at the altimeter. If the pilot should notice a low airspeed, the stick will probably be moved forward, only to be pulled back again when the pilot again looks outside.

As the pilot begins the turn onto what should be the base leg, the glider is flying slowly and the pilot notices the turn must be continued to line up with the runway. There is not enough room for a proper base leg. The pilot becomes apprehensive about using a steep turn at this altitude and resists using enough bank angle.

Instead, the pilot incorrectly presses on the instinctive turning control — the rudder. In our example, the pilot is now holding excessive back stick pressure and excessive left rudder.

The rudder is now causing a skidding turn, resulting in the glider trying to increase its bank angle. To keep the glider from increasing the bank angle, our pilot now uses right aileron pressure. This uncoordinated flight causes an increase in sink rate — our pilot is already too low, so now will hold additional back stick pressure.

At this point, our pilot is holding left rudder and right aileron — crossed controls. In addition, excessive back stick pressure is being used. All of this is the result of built-in, subconscious mechanical reasoning. It is what our subconscious will cause us to do in these high stress situations. The likelihood of an uncontrolled and dangerous stall and spin are great.

As things have progressed, the skidding turn is causing the glider to want to bank more and our pilot is resisting with more and more opposite aileron. The down aileron on the inside wing — the left one in our example — helps to drag that wing back, slowing it down and decreasing its lift which requires more aileron, etc. The resulting uncontrolled roll towards the lowered wing may eventually be so fast, it is possible for the bank to be vertical or even past vertical before it can be stopped.

CAUTION: When practicing crossed-control stalls, it is important to have a safe altitude because of the possible extreme nose-down attitude and resulting loss of altitude.

Before practicing any stalls, check the cockpit for any loose objects and be sure to clear the area for other traffic, especially below you. To adequately clear, you must make two 90 degree turns, a 180 degree turn, or a 360 degree turn.

Fly straight in a normal glide, and trim the aircraft for a normal speed. When the speed is stable, begin to slow down with a slight back stick pressure to a few knots above stall. Roll into a very gentle angle of bank, simulating a pilot who is afraid to use a steeper angle of bank. Now press the rudder in the direction of the turn, attempting to force the turn with rudder. Hold the bank at a constant angle. The glider will want to increase its bank angle, so you will have to add more and more opposite aileron pressure. The sink rate will be increasing and you will hold more and more back stick pressure.

All of the control pressures should be increased until the glider stalls. When the stall occurs, a recovery is made by releasing the control pressures, applying opposite rudder, control stick forward, pausing, and finally rolling level with coordinated control movements. Since the nose will be well down, it won't be necessary to use very much forward stick pressure in the recovery — but don't over do it and regain too much airspeed. Normal airspeed or slightly faster should be sufficient.

In a crossed-control stall, there often is very little warning. Considerably more altitude is lost than with the docile stalls you have been practicing.

It is obvious this type of stall must be avoided — especially close to the ground.

It should be emphasized the scenario we have just described, during any of the five occasions mentioned, is the direct cause of many serious and often fatal glider accidents. You can overcome the statistics by always maintaining proper airspeed — not too fast — not too slow. Always keep the nose of the glider below the horizon, and always fly coordinated (i.e.. using stick and rudder together properly) — **keep the yaw string straight.** Do it especially during low altitude turns.

This maneuver should be practiced with the dive brakes and/or flaps deployed as well as retracted.

CHAPTER 20

SPINS

The object of this maneuver is to enable the pilot to recognize the spin, take prompt, positive actions to prevent its development, and recovery with a minimum loss of altitude. The spiral dive will normally be demonstrated at the same time, so the student can be made aware of the differences in the two maneuvers and recovery procedures.

A spin is described by the FAA as "an aggravated stall that results in what is termed 'auto rotation' wherein the aircraft follows a corkscrew path in a downward direction".

Current FAA rules do not require applicants for private or commercial pilot certificates to be given training in spins. Flight instructor candidates may be asked to demonstrate recovery from spin situations during their flight tests or renewals and therefore will need spin training. Spins continue to be a significant factor in many aircraft accidents, so most flight instructors give their students at least some spin recognition and recovery training.

You should learn the causes of spins — both from glider aerodynamics and human psychological reasoning — and use proper flying techniques to prevent accidental spins from developing. If you couple this knowledge with the ability to make a prompt, positive recovery from any developing spin situation, you will gain a great deal of confidence and be a better, safer pilot.

Some aircraft, including gliders, are specifically placarded against intentional spins. The glider you use for practice must be specifically approved for the spin maneuver. Aircraft in the NORMAL category may not be spun. In fact, the pilot should assume an aircraft certified in the normal category may become uncontrollable in a spin.

Most aircraft in the UTILITY or AEROBATIC categories may be spun, but you must refer to their flight manuals and placards to be sure. The manufacturers of these aircraft are only required to demonstrate a one turn spin and recovery for certification. If you perform more than one turn, you may be doing something that no highly trained factory test pilot has done. The aircraft may not recover from a multi-turn spin!

In the preceding chapter on crossed-control stalls we saw how you might accidentally enter this serious situation, using incorrect reactions. Many modern sailplanes are quite difficult to spin. It may require considerable skill to get a true spin started, let alone be able to maintain a spin through several turns. These same sailplanes may be accidentally put into a spin by mishandling the controls during turns — especially low to the ground. For this reason, it is important for you to practice all the different stalls and flight at minimum controllable airspeed until your ability to recognize an incipient stall, and subsequently make a prompt, positive recovery with proper control responses is fully developed.

During flight at minimum speeds or during a stall, a wing may begin to go down, or 'drop'. When the wing drops, the nose will also begin to yaw towards the lowering wing.

The rudder plays a very important role during a stall. By applying rudder opposite the decsending wing, the nose will be prevented from yawing towards the lowering wing and this will prevent the lowering wing from dropping further before the stall is broken . The spin will be prevented.

If a wing drops during a stall and the nose is permitted to yaw, the aircraft will begin a slip towards the lowered wing. This slip will cause the relative airflow to strike the side of the fuselage and tail. The aircraft will want to "weathervane" into the relative airflow, causing the outboard or high wing to increase its speed, which causes the aircraft to want to bank even more, which causes more sideslip, etc.

The aircraft continues to roll and yaw. It will continue in this state of equilibrium known as autorotation until a recovery is made.

Each glider has its own spinning characteristics which will be partially dependent of the CG location. As long as the glider is within the allowable CG range, you will be able to recover normally. If, however, the CG is aft of the limits, the aircraft may enter a "flat spin" and the recovery may be more difficult, or even impossible.

Some gliders have special spin recovery procedures developed after extensive flight testing. You should always consult the FAA approved flight manual for the proper recovery technique for that particular glider. The following is the suggested standard spin recovery technique as recommended by the FAA:

To recover from a spin, the pilot should first apply full opposite rudder; then after the rotation begins to slow, apply brisk, positive forward movement of the elevator control (forward of the neutral position). There should then be a distinct pause as the glider regains flying speed and the spin rotation stops. The rudder then should be neutralized to prevent a side slip in the opposite direction, and the pilot can then begin to roll level and bring the nose up to level flight.

A timid pilot might use slow, overcautious control movements during the recovery. It has been found such movements may permit some aircraft to continue spinning. Brisk, positive control movements usually result in a more positive, quicker recovery.

After the spinning stops, the sailplane may build up speed rapidly. You should bring the nose of the glider up to prevent over-speeding, and yet you must use some caution not to be too abrupt for fear of causing a secondary stall which could result in another spin. During spin practice, you should have your hand on the dive brake handle in case you need to deploy them to help prevent over-speeding.

NORMAL SPIN RECOVERY

1. **Apply opposite rudder to slow rotation.**

2. **Apply positive forward elevator movement to break the stall.**

3. **Pause.**

4. **Neutralize rudder as spinning stops.**

5. **Return to level flight with coordinated control usage.**

It is important to recognize the following signs during a spin so you can differentiate between a spin and a spiral dive. During most spins the glider will be in a steep nose down attitude. The airspeed will stabilize (but may fluctuate), and the yaw string will be <u>way</u> off center. As you will see in the next section, the signs of a spiral dive are very different. The recovery procedure from a spiral dive is different as well.

If you are going to fly gliders safely, you must be proficient at spin recoveries.

CHAPTER 21

SPIRAL DIVE

You learned in the chapters on stability that an aircraft in a turn weighs more due to centrifugal force. To offset this additional weight, you must hold back on the control stick to provide a higher angle of attack and thus more lift in order to offset the additional weight if you are to keep the airspeed the same.

If you allow the aircraft to bank still steeper, you will have to provide even more back pressure. If the bank angle continues to increase, you will eventually have a bank angle so steep, the control stick will be held fully back against the stop in an attempt to maintain a steady speed.

If you allow the bank angle to increase from this point, the speed will begin to increase. Since the elevator is in the full aft position, the only way the pilot can now prevent the speed from increasing is to reduce the bank angle.

As the speed increases, the lift produced by the wing also increases. This tightens the turn, which causes the aircraft to weigh more, which causes more speed, which causes more lift, etc. This, then, is the spiral dive: A vicious cycle of increasing speed which in a turn causes the aircraft to weigh more until finally the aircraft structure can stand no more and something fails — a wing or the tail or some other structure. The 'G' loads can even build to a point where the pilot passes out.

At no time is the aircraft stalled. The controls all are still working normally with the possible exception of the elevator. In this steep turn with the speed ever increasing, a novice pilot might mistakenly keep pulling back on the stick in a futile attempt to reduce the airspeed.

The culprit then is the bank angle. The recovery is quite simple. Since the wing and ailerons are not stalled, simply apply opposite aileron and rudder together to unbank the glider. As soon as the bank angle is reduced, it is an easy matter to reduce the pitch angle (dive) with the now effective elevator.

CAUTION: If excessive airspeed is developing or has developed during a spiral dive, open the dive brakes in order to help reduce the acceleration and to help prevent over-speeding. Glider certification reqwuirements require the dive brakes to be allowed to be opened up to the maximum red-line speed. While practicing spiral dives, you should not allow the airspeed to go beyond maneuvering speed.

Note the differences of the signs of the spiral dive in comparison with the spin.

Spiral Dive

1. **Nose not as steeply down on the horizon.**

2. **Ever increasing airspeed.**

3. **Yaw string only slightly off center.**

Spin

1. **Nose well below horizon.**

2. **Stable airspeed. (More or less)**

3. **Yaw string extremely deflected.**

Powered airplane pilots who inadvertently fly into clouds where they have no outside visual reference, "flying blind," almost always enter a spiral dive. Many aircraft accidents are the result of inexperienced pilots flying in instrument flight conditions with minimal training and/or instrumentation. It is usually one of those low overcast days with drizzly rain. Witnesses typically report the sound of a high revving engine. When the plane was sighted, it was "in a spin" — actually a spiral dive — sometimes in pieces from structural failure before it struck the ground. It can happen in a glider too!

Do not fly gliders in clouds without proper training and instruments.

Uvalde Texas soaring contest meeting.
Photo by Rosalie Keene

CHAPTER 22

SLIPS

A slip is a descent with one wing lowered and the glider's longitudinal axis aligned at an angle to the flight path. A slip might be used for two purposes: To create extra drag to increase the descent rate without increasing airspeed, and to enable the aircraft to fly a straight ground track while landing in a crosswind by "side-slipping" through the air enough to counteract the drift caused by the wind.

At one time, gliders did not have glide path control devices such as spoilers, dive brakes, and flaps. Pilots used the slip to control where they would touch down. Slips are now used primarily for landings in crosswinds and for clearing tall obstructions during off-field landings. Every so often, a pilot might misjudge the landing approach so severely that he or she must resort to the sideslip in addition to the dive brakes.

The use of slips has limitations. Some pilots may develop the habit of losing altitude with violent slipping rather than with a smooth application of the controls, and exercising good judgment so only a slight or moderate slip is required. In a real emergency, this kind of habit or erratic behavior will eventually lead to trouble because the excessive slipping can easily result in preventing a touchdown anywhere near the intended touchdown point.

A forward slip is a slip in which the gliders direction continues along the same ground path as before the slip. This would be typically used to lose altitude while flying on final with the glider on the proper ground track but too high. If there is a crosswind, the slip will be much more effective if made toward the side from which the wind is blowing. (Windward wing lowered.) Always slip into the wind.

Beginning with the glider in straight glide, the wing on the side toward which the slip is to be made should be lowered by using the ailerons. At the same time, the aircraft's nose must be yawed in the opposite direction by applying opposite rudder. This results in the aircraft's longitudinal axis being at an angle to its original flight path. The amount the nose is yawed in the opposite direction from the bank should be such that the original ground track is maintained. Airspeed must be kept steady by maintaining the same pitch attitude and not allowing the nose to pitch down.

Because of the locations of the pitot tube and static vents, the airspeed indication may have considerable error when the glider is in a slip. You must be aware of this and recognize a properly performed slip by the attitude of the glider, the sound of the airflow, and the feel of the controls.

To discontinue the slip, level the wings with the ailerons and simultaneously release the rudder pressure, while adjusting the stick pressure to maintain a constant airspeed. If you release the rudder pressure too abruptly, the nose will swing too quickly into line or may yaw in the opposite direction and the glider will tend to gain excess speed.

If you are using a slip during the last portions of the landing, you must be careful to align the fuselage of the glider with the runway prior to touchdown so the glider is pointed in the same direction it is traveling over the ground. This requires the pilot to use timely action to discontinue the slip at just the right moment. Failure to do so may result in severe side loads on the undercarriage. It may also result in a violent ground loop, or the glider turning uncontrollably toward the side of the runway.

A sideslip is distinguished from a forward slip only in the fact that in a sideslip the longitudinal axis of the aircraft remains parallel to the original flight path, but the flight path "slips" sideways according to the steepness of the bank. The sideslip is important in counteracting wind drift during crosswind landings.

You may be concerned about the glider being flown in a cross-controlled manner during a slip. Since the airspeed indicator often is erratic and can even read zero airspeed during the slip, you may naturally assume that this is a dangerous flight attitude. As you have found out by now, crossed-control stalls can be very dangerous.

In a crossed-control stall, the aircraft will always drop the wing that has the highest angle of attack, which means the wing with the down aileron. In a slip the aircraft has the down aileron on the high wing, so the high wing would tend to stall first. This is possible, but it also means a stall would take a long time to develop, and you would surely recognize the problem and take action. In addition to the time delay, to recover from a crossed-control stall, you would apply opposite rudder to the rotation. In a slip you are holding rudder pressure opposite the bank angle, so the glider would again have to go "over the top" and rotate in the opposite direction to the slip if it did stall. For your own understanding, you should try stalling the glider from slips so you are aware of how it reacts. Have your instructor demonstrate this, then you try it. Your instructor will keep you out of trouble and correct any flying errors.

There is a particular hazard you should be aware of. Suppose you are on base leg of the landing pattern as depicted on the top of the next page. The wind is blowing across the runway in the direction indicated. You decide you are too high and need to slip. You may be tempted to enter the slip to the right by applying the required left rudder as you turn onto final. This is very dangerous because you are turning left while holding the controls crossed. You are holding rudder pressure in the direction of the turn (the dreaded skidding turn). While turning, entering a sideslip opposite the direction of the turn can lead to a stall-spin because you are holding the controls as necessary to enter a spin. It is generally best to wait until you are lined up on final approach before you initiate a slip.

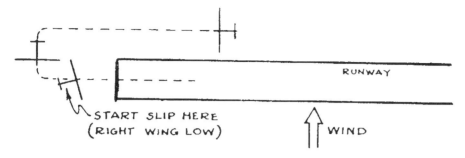

START SLIP HERE
(RIGHT WING LOW)

RUNWAY

WIND

If the wind were blowing from the opposite direction in our example, you would be able to safely enter a slip during the turn onto final because you would be holding the controls in a recover-from-a-turning-stall manner.

CAUTION: As a rule of thumb, avoid entering a slip while in a turn.

You can practice slips at altitude by flying along a road, or fence row while performing a side slip. Try to have a smooth entry and a smooth recovery, while maintaining a steady airspeed. You should be able to side slip left or right equally well.

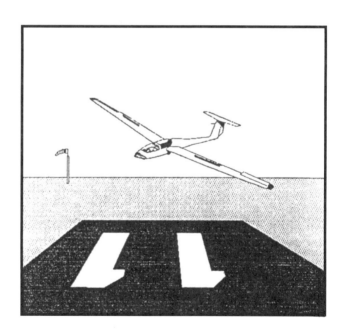

drawn by
Bill McKnight

Filming "The Thomas Crown Affair."
Photo by Andrew Dignan

CHAPTER 23

SPEED TO FLY

There is a best speed-to-fly for nearly every flight situation. Landing pattern speeds, best distance speeds, minimum sinking speeds, best speed to fly in wind, and speeds to fly between thermals are all important to the soaring pilot. During your flight test you will be asked to explain and be able to establish best speeds-to-fly for various conditions.

It is helpful to understand how the manufacturer determines the published speeds-to-fly for a new design. We will go through a possible step-by-step method for a mythical glider.

We would begin with the design criteria we would give the glider's designers for the desired speeds and performance figures. As a builder, we would have told the designers what kind of performance we wanted to have when we were finished, and they would have done their best to come up with a design to fulfill our goals.

After the prototype is built, we would test fly it and measure the actual performance to see how it compares with our goals. We would select a calm morning when the upper air was stable, tow the glider to several thousand feet and begin measuring the sink rate at different airspeeds. Specially calibrated instruments would be used to achieve the most accurate data.

We would measure the glider's sink rate beginning at the slowest possible speed. The following data might evolve:

AIRSPEED (Knots)	SINK RATE (Knots)
40	1.6
45	1.37
50	1.41
55	1.58
60	1.80
65	2.12
70	2.50
75	2.95
80	3.45
85	3.99
90	4.55
95	5.12
100	5.72
110	7.0

We would take this data and transfer it to a graph like the following:

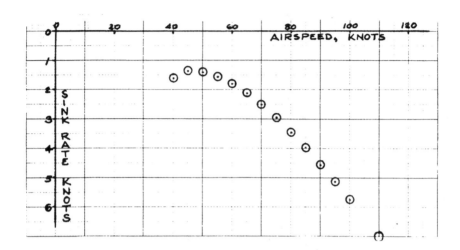

We would then connect the data points and the result would be the performance curve for our glider. This curve is commonly called the aircraft's "POLAR".

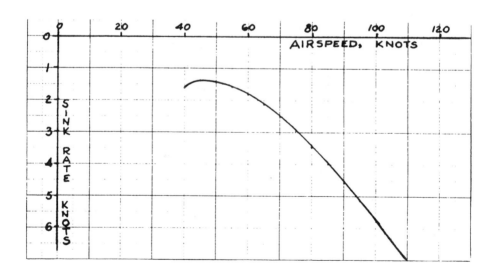

From this polar we can determine several speeds-to-fly for different situations, as well as determining the best performance speeds. The polar begins at the stall speed, (Vs), and ends at the maximum speed for which the glider was tested. This maximum speed is usually the Vd or Maximum Design Speed, and is usually the speed flutter is first detected.

Notice the sink rate for the glider initially decreases as the speed is increased from the stall speed. The speed the glider sinks at the slowest rate, or minimum sinking speed is at the highest point on the polar, several miles an hour faster than the stall speed. Pilots subconsciously fly too slowly when they are trying to achieve a fast climb rate in thermals. To achieve the fastest climb rate, a pilot must fly faster than the slowest speed the glider will fly.

We now have three of the 'working' speeds of our glider:

Stall speed - 40 knots
Minimum sink - 46 knots
Maximum speed -110 knots

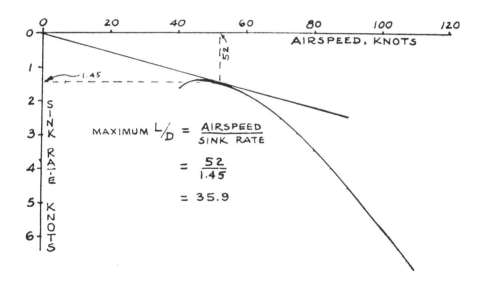

BEST GLIDE SPEED

The next speed we will determine will be the 'best glide' or best L/D speed. This is easily done by drawing a line from the intersection of the speed and sink lines, tangent to the polar, as in the previous drawing:

From the point where the tangential line touches the polar, we draw a line up to the velocity line and over to the sink line. We then divide the sink rate into the velocity to obtain the best glide angle, or max L/D. In this example we find our glider has a max L/D of 35.9, by dividing 52 by 1.45. We can obtain the L/D for any other airspeed by marking the polar at any speed and then dividing that speed by the corresponding sink rate.

If we would compute the L/D for any other point on the polar, the performance will be less than max L/D. The angle the tangential line makes with the speed line is the glide angle if the drawing was to scale. (Angle shown is off by a factor of 10).

SPEEDS TO FLY WITH WIND

If you are flying to a point on the ground, such as the final glide of the day, you will have to take into consideration the wind. If you have a head wind, you should fly faster. A tail wind will call for a slower speed. To understand this, imagine flying into a 52 knot head wind. Our mythical glider has a best L/D of 35.9 to one at 52 knots. If we flew into this head wind at best L/D speed we would not make any progress over the ground. The glider would descend vertically. To make forward progress we would have to fly at a speed above the best L/D speed to penetrate into the wind. If we slowed to 40 knots, we would fly backwards 12 knots!

The polar can give us the best speed-to-fly for any wind condition. Draw a line from the wind speed, (+ or -), tangent to the polar to derive the corresponding speed-to-fly. Originating the tangential line from a point along the airspeed line has the same affect as displacing the polar to reflect the effect of wind.

(See drawing on next page)

One important rule-of-thumb can be derived from this graph: Simply add 1/2 of any head wind, or subtract 1/4 of any tail wind to the speed ring speed-to-fly indication. Can you see from the graph why tail winds have little effect on the best speed-to-fly? Hint: It has to do with the curve of the polar.

SPEED-TO-FLY THROUGH SINKING AIR

When flying from one thermal to the next, it is normal to encounter sinking air. The optimum speed-to-fly depends on the amount of sink encountered. It is important to realize the basic rule: Speed up in sink, slow down in lift. How much to speed up in sink is determined from the polar.

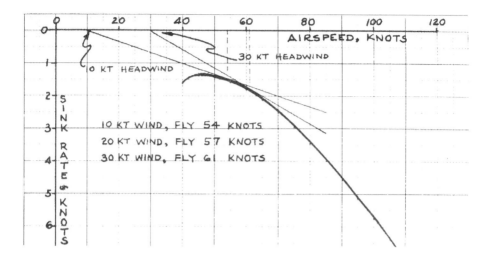

The polar on the graph shows the sink rate of the glider flying in still air. If the glider is flying through sinking air, then the polar of the glider would have to be lowered down the graph the amount the air is sinking. Instead of doing this, we can simply raise the originating point to equal the sinking rate of the air mass above the polar to achieve the same result. The graph below shows our glider flying through a sinking air mass of 2.8 knots (about the same as 280 feet per minute).

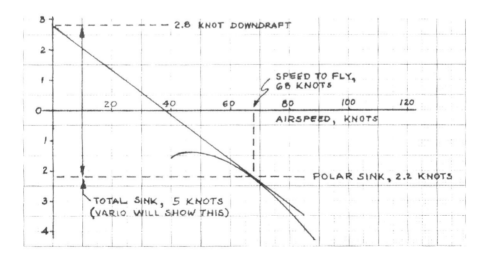

The tangential line is drawn from a point 2.8 knots above the intersection, which is the same as lowering the polar down 2.8 knots. We now obtain the speed-to-fly for this sink rate of 68 knots. If we draw similar lines for other sink rates, we can develop another table for speeds-to-fly for any sink rate.

Aerotow
Photo by Rosalie Keene

SINK RATE (KNOTS)	SPEED TO FLY
0	52
.5	55
1.0	57
1.5	60
2.0	63
2.5	66
3.0	70
3.5	72
4.0	75
5.0	84
6.0	89

SPEED-TO-FLY CALCULATIONS CONSIDERING THERMAL STRENGTH

The faster you are able to climb, the faster the potential average cross-country ground speeds can be. If the lift is strong, you should fly faster between thermals. The mathematical proof of this point is beyond the scope of this book, but consider the following drawing:

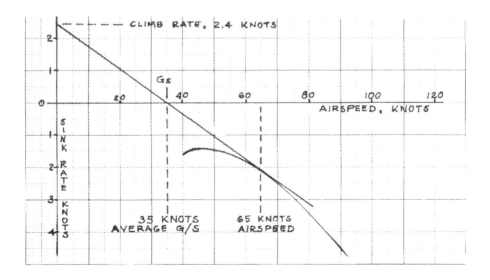

This graph is the same as the previous one explaining speed-to-fly considering the sink rate of the air mass. In this new graph there is a new fact indicated by the letters G/S which shows the ground speed achieved with this particular climb rate. G/S is the point the tangential line crosses the horizontal velocity line. As the climb rate increases, the point G/S would move further and further to the right. The faster you can climb, the faster the achievable ground speed.

When flying from one thermal to the next, you should combine the speed-to-fly for the rate of climb you expect with the speed-to-fly considering the rate of sink you are experiencing as you fly from one thermal to the next in order to to achieve the fastest ground speed. This next graph combines both the climb rate with the sink rate to give the speed-to-fly for that circumstance.

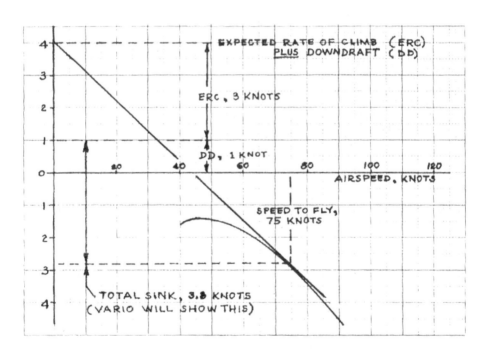

THE SPEED RING

Once we have this information, we would need to put it into a useful form. We could simply fasten the graphs and tables to the instrument panel and refer to them, or we could make a speed-to-fly ring. (No, not for your finger). The information from the graphs and tables would be used to make a rotatable ring installed on the face of the variometer. This ring was invented by Dr. Paul MacCready, Jr. It is called a speed-to-fly ring, or simply speed ring. A datum mark is set opposite the zero mark on the variometer scale, and the speeds-to-fly for the corresponding rates of sink plus the sink rate of the glider from the table are marked on the ring.

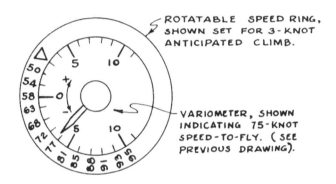

ROTATABLE SPEED RING, SHOWN SET FOR 3-KNOT ANTICIPATED CLIMB.

VARIOMETER, SHOWN INDICATING 75-KNOT SPEED-TO-FLY. (SEE PREVIOUS DRAWING).

With the speed ring, we would then be able to have a quick, convenient reference to determine the best speed-to-fly for the air mass condition we are experiencing at the moment.

To take into consideration the climb rate of the thermals you are using, the speed ring is simply rotated to the rate of climb you are expecting, and then the speed-to-fly between thermals is read directly from where the variometer needle is pointing as you pass through sinking air.

The speed ring should be used as a guide while flying from one thermal to the next. It is not practical to change the airspeed every time the variometer twitches. An average speed-to-fly between thermals should be sought for optimum performance. A pilot who constantly changes airspeed will probably confuse the instrumentation, and actually fly a greater distance than the pilot who simply flies a steady speed.

A pilot who flies with a speed ring setting 50% too low, will still net a speed only slightly slower than the pilot who sets the speed ring precisely correct.

(See drawing next page)

IMPORTANT NOTE: When flying from thermal to thermal, wind doesn't affect the speed-to-fly computations. Wind only affects the speed-to-fly when the glider is flying to a point on the ground.

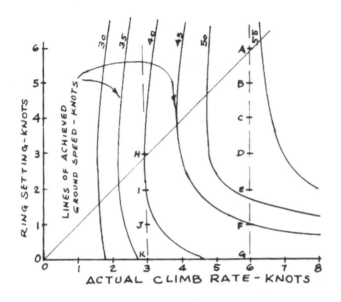

FINAL GLIDE CALCULATORS

Armed with our calculations and charts, we are now ready to do battle with the elements. Well, almost. We need to reduce this pile of information to a more usable form.

Consider the following problem:

Your glider has a maximum glide ratio of 42 to 1 at 47 knots. You are at 2,000 feet above your goal in a thermal lifting you at the rate of four knots. You are 20 nautical miles from the goal. There is no wind. How high should you climb? How fast should you fly?

You could:

A. Climb to 3200 above ground level (AGL) and fly at 60 knots with a glide ratio of 38:1.

B. Climb to 3800 AGL and fly at 71 knots with a glide ratio of 32:1.

C. Climb to 5067 AGL and fly at 84 knots with a glide ratio of 24:1.

D. Climb to 5527 AGL and fly at 90 knots with a glide ratio of 22:1.

E. Climb to 6422 AGL and fly at 100 knots with a glide ratio of 19:1.

Simple arithmetic gives us the following total elapsed times for each possibility: (1 knot = approximately 101.3 feet per minute.)

CLIMB TIME	GLIDE TIME	TOTAL TIME
A. 2.96	20	22.96 Minutes
B. 4.44	16.9	21.34 Minutes
C. 6.41	14.3	20.71 Minutes
D. 8.70	13.33	22.03 Minutes
E. 10.91	12.0	22.91 Minutes

The quickest time is C. Climb to 5067 feet and fly 84 knots. (You would also add a safety factor and enough altitude for a safe landing pattern in a real final glide problem).

Several handy cockpit final glide calculators are available, or you can make your own. There are even electronic final glide computers. Shown is a JSW final glide calculator made in England for a glider with a 42:1 L/D. (25:1 at 80 knots).

At the top of the calculator is a scale indicating what speed-to-fly at different achieved rates of climb. This scale indicates you should fly 84 knots if you are achieving a four knot climb rate as in our example.

Set the calculator by rotating the center dial so 84 knots is aligned with the wind speed. Since there is no wind in our problem, set the 84 knot speed on the 0 wind speed line. To allow for any wind, set the 84 knot speed on the appropriate wind line and then read off the altitude needed. Now you are ready to read the altitude to climb for any distance.

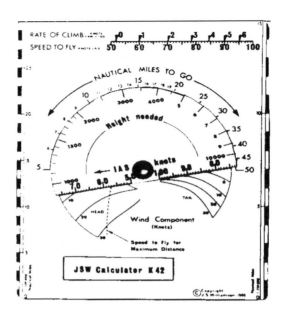

Our problem was for a distance of 20 nautical miles, and the calculator for this glider indicates the needed altitude is 4600 feet.

What if the thermals did not go as high as 4600 feet? Answer: Climb in your present thermal and fly at 84 knots (in our example) to the next thermal and recompute the altitude needed from this new distance until you are within reach of the goal.

What if you are 20 nautical miles from your goal, and you can't climb to the 4600 feet needed, and you suspect there are no more thermals? Answer: Rotate the dial so your height is opposite the mileage to go, and then read the speed-to-fly at the wind speed line. This gives the best speed-to-fly to cover the distance in the least amount of time, as long as you are within gliding range of the goal.

The ability to make final glide calculations is important for cross-country flying and competition soaring. It is important to practice using the final glide calculator to gain confidence in what it tells you.

HOW HIGH DO I NEED TO BE TO MAKE IT HOME?

Sooner or later you will be faced with the problem of figuring out how high you need to be to fly a certain distance considering wind but without the use of a flight calculator.

Consider this problem: You are flying a glider with a glide ratio of 30:1 at a speed of 52 m.p.h.. You are 13 miles away from your home gliderport and you are flying into a 10 m.p.h. head wind. How high do you need to be?

A final glide computer will give the answer (if you have a calculator for a glider of that performance), but you should be able to figure out the answer using simple math.

Here is one of those formulas you should memorize, or at least know where to find it if you ever need it. Flight examiners often will ask you to perform these calculations on the oral part of the flight test.

$$Gag = Gaa \frac{(airspeed + or- wind)}{airspeed}$$

Where Gag = Glide angle over the ground.
    Gaa = Glide angle in the air.

Substituting the information from the problem gives us:

$$Gag = 30 \left(\frac{52 - 10}{52} \right) = 30 \times .81 = 24.3$$

The glide ratio of the glider into a 10 m.p.h. head wind is reduced to 24.3:1

Dividing 5280 (the number of feet in a mile) by 24.3 gives us the number of feet lost per mile, or in this case, 217 feet per mile. We can now multiply any number of miles times 217 and obtain how high we need to be. We would also need to add a safety factor and enough altitude to perform a safe landing pattern.

CHAPTER 24

THE LOADING CHART

The competent pilot must have a good understanding of the forces acting on an aircraft in flight and the operating limitations of any particular aircraft he or she is flying.

A *load factor* is the ratio of the total air load acting on the aircraft to the gross weight of the aircraft. For example, a load factor of 3 means the total load on the aircraft's structure is three times its gross weight. We usually express these load factors in terms of "G"; that is, a load factor of 3 is spoken of as 3 G's, or 3 Gravities.

When you dive the glider and then pull back on the stick to produce a load factor of 3 G's, you will be pressed down into the seat with a force equal to three times your weight. You get a very real idea of the magnitude of the load factor by considering the amount you are being pressed down into the seat. Since the amount of pressure required to move the control surfaces varies with different gliders and many gliders have well balanced controls, you should not attempt to judge how much load you are exerting on the airframe by the amount of control "feel" you are experiencing.

Aircraft are designed to withstand only a certain amount of load. If the designers were forced to design the aircraft to withstand the kinds of forces existing in a tropical thunderstorm or the kind of loads a pilot can put on the aircraft by abusive use of the controls, it would have to be built so strong and would weigh so much, it would not be a practical aircraft.

How strong an aircraft is built is determined by the kinds of use it will be subjected to. Pilots can make very hard landings, or by jerking on the controls abruptly, create very high G loads. These extreme loads have to be disregarded if we are to have aircraft that will carry reasonably payloads, land slowly, etc.

Over the years, designers have established a set of reasonable limits to be expected in what are considered normal operations. These load factors are called "limit load factors". Federal Aviation Regulations require the aircraft structure to withstand 1 1/2 times these limits without failure. Parts of the structure may bend or be distorted and some damage may occur, but the structure should not fail entirely.

This safety factor is built into the aircraft because of unknown variables in material and manufacturing processes. You should never willfully abuse the normal operating limits.

GUST LOAD FACTORS

Gust load factor requirements are essentially the same today as they have been for many years. Millions of hours of safe aircraft operations have proven them to be adequate. A *standard weak gust* is considered to be 25 feet per second by OSTIV (Organization Scientifique et Technique de Vol a' Voile, an international governing body), and a *standard strong gust* is 50 feet per second. A glider must be able to withstand the weak gust up to its *maximum design speed* (Vd) and a strong gust up to its *maximum maneuvering speed* (Va).

A pilot cannot control the intensity of the gusts ahead, but can often predict strong, turbulent conditions such as a thunderstorm or dust devils ahead, and reduce the aircraft's speed.

Gusts can and do come from any direction. There are side gusts, up gusts and down gusts. Side gusts are seldom any problem, but up and down gusts can be of great consequence. An up or down gust produces additional loads on the wing and spar of the aircraft. As the speed increases, the loads imposed on the aircraft by a gust increase.

The load factor of a glider at rest or undisturbed straight flight is 1 (one). As the speed increases, the load factor imposed on the aircraft by a gust increases.

When an up gust strikes the bottom of the wing, it causes the angle of attack to increase. If a gust is sufficiently strong, the resulting increase in the angle of attack of the wing will cause it to stall. If the glider is flying just above stall speed in level flight, the load factor cannot increase beyond 1 because any increase in angle of attack will cause the wing to stall.

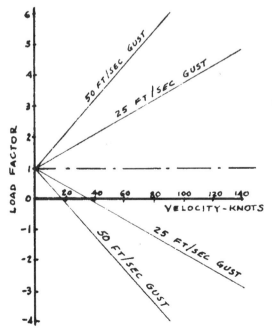

LOAD FACTORS IMPOSED WHEN ENCOUNTERING GUSTS IN A GLIDER.

117

These graphs are for a new aircraft. As it becomes older it will not be able to withstand the forces of a brand new aircraft.

MANEUVERING LOAD FACTORS

In the United States, aircraft are licensed in *categories*, including normal, utility, and acrobatic. The maximum safe load factors specified in the various categories are as follows:

Normal (1)...+3.8 to -1.52.
Utility (mild acrobatics, including spins).... +4.4 to -1.76.
Acrobatic ... +6.0 to -3.0.

(1) For airplanes with a gross weight of more than 4,000 pounds, the limit load factor is reduced.

When a glider is flying straight and level, the load factor is essentially one (1.0). When it is maneuvering, such as turning, the vertical component of lift must be equal to the weight and the total lift therefore is greater than the weight of the glider at rest. The load factors for various angles of bank are given in the following table:

Angle of bank in degrees	0	15	30	45	60	75	80	85	90
Load factor	1.0	1.04	1.15	1.41	2.0	3.86	5.76	11.47	infinity

The following chart shows how rapidly the load factor increases as the bank angle approaches a 90 degree bank angle. A 90 degree banked, constant speed, coordinated turn is mathematically impossible. An aircraft can pass through 90 degrees as in a barrel roll and some acrobatic aircraft are capable of what is called knife-edge flight by using their fuselage to produce lift, but it is not coordinated flight either.

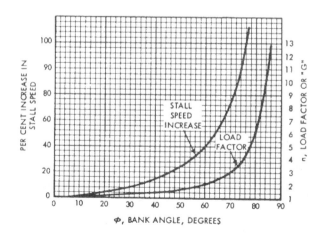

The load factor is increased in any curved flight. Diving and then pulling back on the control stick to make the glider climb produces curved flight and increased positive load factors.

It is also possible to produce negative load factors. While flying upside down the aircraft is producing -1 G's. Pushing forward on the control stick, while flying right side up can also produce negative load factors.

Negative G's beyond -2 are quite dangerous because of physiological problems. Positive G's up to +5 for a brief period can normally be tolerated.

An aircraft may be in a stalled condition at any airspeed. When the critical angle of attack is exceeded, the smooth, laminar airflow over the airfoil breaks up and separates, producing a sudden loss of lift, which results in a stall. There is a certain stalling speed for each load factor. This new stalling speed will be the percentage of the square root of the load factor. In a 60 degree angle of bank, the load factor is 2.0. The square root of two is 1.41, so the stall speed increases by 41% in a 60 degree bank. The maximum speed at which an aircraft may be stalled safely is called the "design maneuvering speed." (Point 'A' and point 'G' in the following diagram).

In the following diagram, the curved line beginning at the left edge and at the 0 load factor, and arcing upward and downward to points 'A' and 'G', is the maximum load factor before the glider stalls for positive and negative load factors at different airspeeds. Point 'A' and 'G' are the maximum load factors which the glider is designed to withstand.

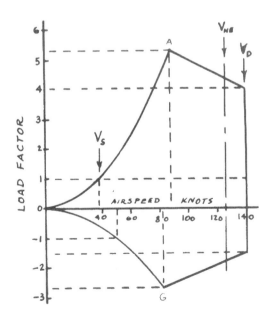

Understanding load factors induced by varying degrees of bank and the significance of maneuvering speed, (Va) will help you prevent two of the most serious types of accidents:

1. Stalls from steep turns or excessive maneuvering near the ground.

2. Structural failures during aerobatics or other violent maneuvers.

The vertical line at the extreme right side of the diagram is the Maximum Design airspeed, (Vd). Pilots understand large loads are not to be applied at high speeds. The maximum load factor is therefore reduced at Vd. Vne, or never exceed speed is an arbitrary 10% reduction from Vd.

Weight is a measure of the the earth's gravity upon something. We express this in pounds, ounces, kilograms, etc.

Gravity is the enemy of aviation. Wings generate lift to offset the weight of an aircraft. Since the amount of lift the wings can create is limited, so too is the weight of the aircraft.

Excessive weight can seriously affect the performance of an aircraft. An overloaded glider will have the following important performance deficiencies:

> Longer takeoff roll.
> Higher takeoff speed.
> Reduced climb rate.
> Reduced climb angle on tow.
> Reduced maneuverability.
> Higher stall speed.
> Higher landing speed.
> Longer landing roll out.

The glider's flight manual will tell you the maximum weight permitted for the glider. Often there is a placard in the cockpit to inform the pilot some or all of the following information: Empty weight, gross weight (maximum weight), minimum pilot weight, maximum pilot weight, etc.

Addition of equipment — radios, instruments, oxygen equipment, — plus repairs or modifications usually add to the original weight of the glider. When equipment changes or repairs are made, the aircraft must be re-weighed to determine its new empty weight, which will affect the useful load. (Useful load is the entire load put aboard an aircraft, including fuel, oil, crew, passengers, water ballast, armament, etc. Useful load is equal to the difference between the actual gross weight and the empty weight of the aircraft.)

BALANCE - CENTER OF GRAVITY

Balance refers to the location of an aircraft's center of gravity (C.G.). C.G. is the point about which an aircraft would balance if it were possible to support the aircraft at that point. It is the mass center of the aircraft, or the point at which the entire weight of the aircraft is concentrated.

If the mass center of the aircraft is displaced too far forward on the longitudinal axis, a nose-heavy condition will result. If, on the other hand, the mass center is too far aft, a tail-heavy condition will result.

Any aircraft must be balanced properly in order for it to be stable and controllable in flight. Generally speaking, an aircraft becomes less controllable as the center of gravity is moved aft, especially at slow speeds. A glider that normally recovers cleanly from stalls and spins may fail to respond when the C.G. is aft of the allowable limits.

A C.G. too far forward may make it impossible to land at a slow airspeed. The glider will also stall at a higher airspeed, be more difficult to take off, and have decreased performance.

Each aircraft has required weight and balance information in the flight manual and/or separate weight and balance records on board for the use of the pilot.

Note: Center of gravity measurement s are performed with the glider properly leveled. See glider flight manuals for "leveling data".

TERMINOLOGY AND DEFINITIONS (ALPHABETICALLY)

1. ARM (MOMENT ARM) is the horizontal distance in inches from the reference datum line to the center of gravity of the item. The algebraic sign is plus (+) if measured aft of the datum, and minus (-) if measured forward of the datum.

2. CENTER OF GRAVITY (C.G.) is the point about which an aircraft would balance if it were possible to suspend it at that point. It is the mass center of the aircraft, or the theoretical point at which the entire weight of the aircraft is assumed to be concentrated. It may be expressed in percent of MAC (mean aerodynamic chord) or in inches from a reference point.

3. CENTER OF GRAVITY LIMITS are the specified forward and aft or lateral points beyond which the C.G. must not be located during takeoff, flight or landing. These limits are indicated on pertinent FAA aircraft type certificate data sheets, specifications, or weight and balance records, and meet the requirements of Federal Aviation Regulations.

4. CENTER OF GRAVITY RANGE is the distance between the forward and aft C.G. limits indicated on pertinent aircraft specifications.

5. DATUM (reference datum) is an imaginary vertical plane or line from which all measurements are taken. The manufacturer establishes the datum. Once the datum has been selected, all moment arms and the location of permissible C.G. range must be taken with reference to that point.

6. MEAN AERODYNAMIC CHORD (MAC) is the average distance from the leading edge to the trailing edge of the wing. The MAC is specified for the aircraft by determining the average chord of an imaginary wing, which has the same aerodynamic characteristics as the actual wing.

7. MOMENT is the product of the weight of an item multiplied by its arm. Moments are commonly expressed in pound-inches (lb.-in.) or inch-pounds. Total moment is the weight of the aircraft multiplied by the distance between the datum and the C.G.

8. STATION is a location in the aircraft, which is identified by a number designating its distance in inches or millimeters from the datum. The datum, is considered as station zero. The station and arm are usually identical. (An item located at station +50 would have an arm of 50 inches).

9. USEFUL LOAD is the weight of the pilot, passengers, baggage, etc. It is the empty weight subtracted from the maximum allowable takeoff weight.

10. WEIGHT, MAXIMUM TAKEOFF is the maximum weight allowable at the start of the takeoff. The takeoff weight for a particular flight may be limited to a lesser weight when runway length, atmospheric conditions, towplane power, or other variables are adverse.

In gliders, the primary concern is with longitudinal, or fore and aft balance. Lateral , or side-to-side balance usually only becomes a concern when water ballast is carried in the wings. Lateral balance is not normally computed, but a pilot must be aware any lateral imbalance can make a hazardous condition for takeoff and landings in particular. Pilots who load water ballast in their wings will be seen to carefully check the lateral balance before takeoff.

C.G. limits are established by the aircraft's manufacturer. The limits are published in the aircraft's FAA Type Certificate Data Sheet or Specifications. If you compute the weight and balance and the C.G. falls outside the allowable limits, you must shift the load or add or subtract weight before flight is attempted.

The forward C.G. limit is usually established by the landing characteristics of the glider. You may be able to fly the glider safely in normal flying situations with a C.G. forward of the limits, but during the landing you may damage the aircraft. This is because the elevator may not have enough force to counter the nose-heavy condition at slow landing speeds.

The aft C.G. limit is the most rearward position that can exist and still have a controllable glider. As the C.G. moves aft, a less stable condition occurs, which decreases the ability of the aircraft to right itself after maneuvering or disturbances by gusts.

COMPUTING WEIGHT AND BALANCE

A simple weight check should first be done before flight. This check will determine if the total weight is below the maximum permitted. Remember to level the glider per the approved flight manual.

SAMPLE WEIGHT AND BALANCE PROBLEM
FOR A GROB G102 CLUB ASTIR

Empty weight	573 lbs.
Maximum permissible weight	838 lbs.
Pilot's weight including parachute	190 lbs.
Barograph, drinking water	3 lbs.

Total weight = 573 + 190 + 3 = 766 lbs.

In this sample problem the total weight is 72 pounds under the maximum permissible weight, so the total weight is OK.

Now we will check to see where the C.G. is located. From the FAA approved flight manual we find the permitted C.G. position is from 12.2 inches to 18.9 inches behind (aft) of the datum. The datum line in this case is the front edge of the wing at the root rib.

We also find in the flight manual the position of the empty C.G. behind the datum is 30.4 inches, and the pilot's C.G. is 22.5 in front of the datum line. Because the pilot sits forward of the datum, this number is a negative number. The emergency kit and drinking water are on the baggage shelf and therefore are on the C.G. of this particular glider; they have a "0" arm.

We can now form a chart from this information. Most flight manuals have a chart you can use for this purpose.

	WEIGHT	ARM	MOMENT
Glider empty weight	573	30.4	17419.2
Pilot and chute	190	-22.5	-4275.0
Emergency kit and water	3	0	0.0
Total	766		13,144.2

You must know two formulas to compute weight and balance:

WEIGHT X ARM = MOMENT

TOTAL MOMENT Divided by TOTAL WEIGHT = C.G.

In our example we added the weights to obtain the total weight of the glider with pilot and gear. This equals 766 pounds.

We also added the total moments, carefully subtracting the negative value for the pilot who is sitting in front of the datum line. This equals 13,144.2 inch-pounds.

From the formula, we now divide the total moment by the total weight to derive the C.G. 13,144.2 divided by 766 = 17.16 inches.

17.16 falls between the allowable C.G. range of 12.2 to 18.9 inches, so we are within the limits and can safely fly in this configuration.

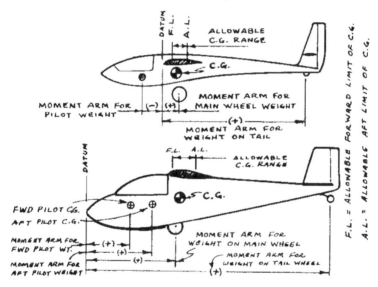

We have just completed a computation method of figuring the weight and balance for this glider. It is common for gliders to have a simple placard in the cockpit to assure the pilot falls within the weight and balance limitations. The following information might be included in such a placard for our sample sailplane, the Grob Club Astir:

PAYLOAD (pilot and parachute)

minimum payload 154 lbs.
maximum payload of 242 lbs.

The maximum weight must not be exceeded.

124

The placard might also explain if you weigh less than the minimum, you should add a factory ballast weight in the place provided, or add weight to the seat. This placard explains as long as you, your clothes, and your parachute weight a total amount between 154 and 242 pounds, the glider will fall within the allowable C.G. limits.

The last technique is the graph method to check if you are within weight and balance limits. One problem with the graph method is the graph is seldom upgraded to reflect equipment changes or weight changes the result of repairs. Be very cautious the graph you use really applies to the particular aircraft you are flying.

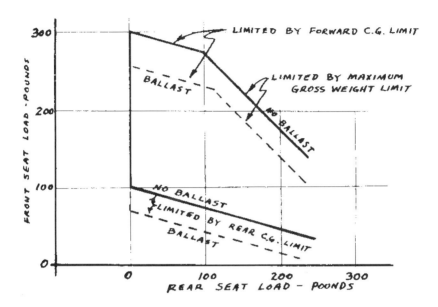

The previous graph is for a Schweizer 2-33. Assuming you are the front pilot and weigh 150 lbs, and your passenger in the rear seat weighs 180 lbs and you are not carrying the optional factory ballast weight — are you within the allowable limits?

From calculations, you should have determined you are within the limits.

Schempp-Hirth Duo Discus
photo by Andrew Dignan

CHAPTER 25

THERMALLING

The ability to soar, means the ability to stay aloft. There are several forms of lift in the atmosphere, but the most common is thermals. Thermals can be thought of as columns of warm air created by the sun heating the surface of the earth. Sailplanes and soaring birds are often seen to circle silently within the boundaries of the column of lift and rise almost effortlessly.

The ability to find and use this form of lift is the basic skill you must develop in order to enjoy the thrills of soaring flight.

A thermal is usually an invisible column of rising air. Sometimes it is revealed as a column of spinning, whirling dust rising off the ground, or sometimes leaves, newspapers and cornstalks give evidence of the solar powered energy source. As you glide through the air, you will encounter turbulence caused by the instability of the air, and sometimes feel a surge of lift as the sailplane rises against you when it encounters a thermal. The instrument showing if the sailplane is rising or sinking is the variometer.

A beginner often turns too soon when lift is encountered. This causes the glider to immediately leave the thermal. Thinking a turn was made in the wrong direction, the pilot then tries a turn in the opposite direction. No lift is found in this direction and the pilot logically assumes it was only a small bump rather than a real thermal. Several minutes and several bumps later the pilot is sitting on the ground while others are still aloft.

(See top drawing on next page)

It's important to fly well into the thermal before making the first turn. Wait a minimum of three seconds after encountering lift before beginning the turn. Five seconds is often better.

(See lower drawing on next page)

WHICH WAY TO TURN

If another sailplane is circling in the thermal you are joining, you must circle in the same direction. It makes no difference if the other sailplane is higher or lower than you. With experience, you will learn how to read evidence in cumulus clouds to help you decide just where to go and which direction to turn.

With no visual clues, simply turn in the direction you think the center of the thermal is. If you turn the wrong direction, simply continue turning until the thermal is encountered again.

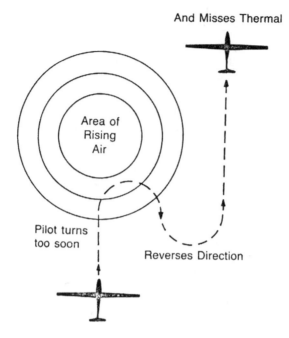

And Misses Thermal

Area of
Rising
Air

Pilot turns
too soon

Reverses Direction

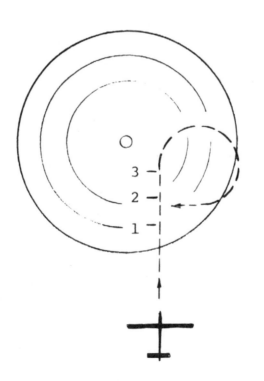

3 —
2 —
1 —

It is important to continue circling in the same direction once you have begun to thermal. It is very difficult to form an idea of what exact shape a thermal is. (They are seldom round.) Reversing the thermalling direction usually finds the glider pilot 'lost' trying to relocate the center or core of the thermal.

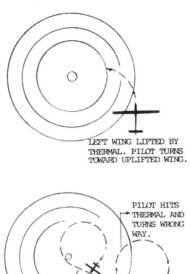

LEFT WING LIFTED BY
THERMAL. PILOT TURNS
TOWARD UPLIFTED WING.

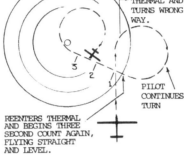

PILOT HITS
THERMAL AND
TURNS WRONG
WAY.

PILOT
CONTINUES
TURN

REENTERS THERMAL
AND BEGINS THREE
SECOND COUNT AGAIN,
FLYING STRAIGHT
AND LEVEL.

CENTERING

A thermal usually will have a core of stronger lift. For the best rate of climb, you should position the glider in this core. This is done by flying straight and level for three seconds whenever you encounter stronger lift, then resuming the turn. A series of adjustments such as this will guide the sailplane to the core.

(See drawing next page)

BANK ANGLE AND AIRSPEED

A sailplane's minimum sink rate occurs when it is flying straight and level. As the glider begins a turn, centrifugal force makes it weigh more, and the sink rate increases. The steeper the bank angle, the higher the sink rate. For this reason, you don't want to bank the glider any steeper than necessary to stay in the best part of the thermal. It is seldom necessary to use a bank angle of more than forty five degrees to remain in the core of most thermals. Steeper angles of bank are used when the thermal is small. Thermals expand as they gain altitude, so a glider pilot would use shallower bank angles at higher altitudes. A thirty degree angle of bank is probably the most often used by pilots while thermalling.

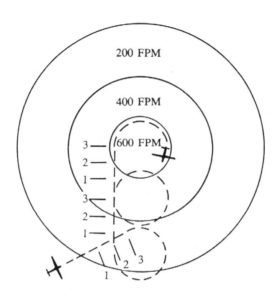

Proper thermalling airspeed will usually be several miles per hour or knots above stall speed. The flight manual will indicate the minimum sinking speed for the glider. This minimum sinking speed occurs in straight and level flight, at the minimum flying weight. Minimum sinking speed increases if the flying weight is above the minimum allowable, and as the bank angle is increased. Typical sailplanes climb best using 45 to 50 knots airspeed. If the thermal is turbulent, a faster airspeed will be desirable for better control of the glider. It is not unusual for a heavy sailplane to thermal at 60 knots. (One knot equals 1.15 m.p.h.. 60 knots = 69 m.p.h..)

You should develop the ability to fly round circles using a constant angle of bank and a constant airspeed for efficient thermalling. Thermals are abstract objects and the best way to deal with an unknown is to form a base that you know is true, and work form that base. The 'base' when dealing with an abstract thermal is a round circle which you are able to shift around until you find the core.

SAFETY

As a low time glider pilot, do not attempt thermalling at low altitudes or near the airport traffic pattern. One thousand feet above ground level (AGL) is a reasonable minimum thermalling altitude for student pilots in most situations. Circumstances at your airport may make it necessary to raise this minimum. Ask your instructor for guidance on this matter.

If you are below 1,000 feet and find a thermal, you should land, explain to the tow pilot where the thermal was, and ask to be taken there at a safe altitude on the next aero tow.

130

MORE ABOUT THERMALLING

The basic thermalling technique is to fly straight for three seconds whenever you encountered lift, or better lift, then circle again using a constant rate of turn. We will now take a more detailed look at a thermal and show you a faster way to find, and stay in the center of a thermal.

A thermal is an invisible thing. We can't see it, so we deal with it by making some assumptions. We generally think of a thermal as being a rising column of air, tilted with the wind.

It is useful to consider how a thermal is born, and what a thermal might look like. A thermal is rising warm air. The sun's rays pass through the air without heating it significantly. When the sun's radiational energy strikes the earth, this energy is converted to heat. The air is warmed by contact with some warm surface. Most thermals are created over the earth, especially cultivated farm fields. Other good thermal sources include large parking lots, factories, and towns.

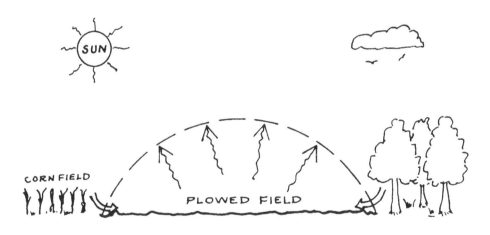

Eventually, the air above the field is warmed enough so it becomes buoyant. The air rises as a bubble of warmed, less dense air and as the bubble rises, it is replaced by cooler air from surrounding fields and woods.

A thermal begins its life as a series of bubbles of rising air. In fact, many thermals are only a series of bubbles of rising air. These bubbles rise at different rates, and are drifted downwind. The bubbles react with the bubbles preceding them by engulfing, or sliding by, or joining up in a chain-like fashion. The thermal rises and rapidly cools and becomes less able to hold its moisture in the invisible state. The moisture condenses and becomes visible as a cumulus cloud if there is enough moisture, and the condensation level is below the level at which the thermal temperature reaches equilibrium.

A thermal should be thought of as being like a chimney built by a drunken mason, rather than a column. In fact, you might notice how seldom you can make more than a few turns in a thermal before you find you need to make an adjustment. A good pilot is constantly paying attention to the variometer signals, and very frequently making slight adjustments to the glider's circles in order to stay within the very best part of the thermal bubble.

Let's take a look at a typical thermal bubble.

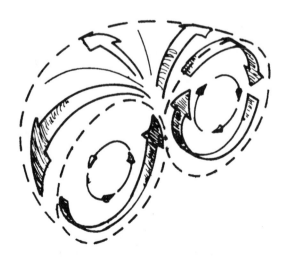

132

The inner core is the most buoyant part of the rising bubble. The inner core rises until it meets the cooler, more dense ambient air at the top of the bubble where it is cooled and then flows downward (actually the bubble rises past it) along the outside of the bubble. The air flowing down the outside of the bubble is interacting with the ambient air and is quite turbulent. This explains why it is common to experience an increased sink rate and turbulence when approaching a thermal.

THERMAL INDICATORS

There often are excellent indicators of where thermals exist. Other circling sailplanes, soaring birds, dust devils, even debris such as leaves and paper can show the presence of thermals.

By far the most common indicators of thermal activity are cumulus clouds. However, there are three types of cumulus clouds: Building, dissipating, and mature. We want to fly towards the building clouds. Look for those with dark bases, sharper, distinct contours and triangular shape. Ragged edges usually mean the thermal is dying.

If you are relatively high, you should concentrate primarily on the clouds for indications of possible lift. At lower altitudes, you will need to look at ground features for clues of thermal sources. Keep a lookout for other sailplanes or birds for thermal markers.

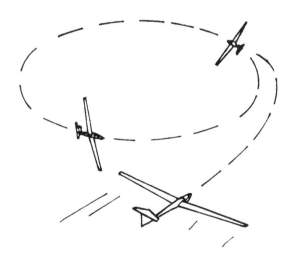

ENTERING THERMALS

It is common to encounter increased sink as you near a thermal, followed by a zone of turbulence. Next, you will often notice the airspeed increases suddenly, and then you will feel a surge and the variometer will show a climb.

Thermals near the gliding site, or on course line at a contest are often occupied by one or more sailplanes. Rules have been developed to help prevent collisions:

1. The first glider to enter the thermal establishes the circling direction for all others who enter the thermal later regardless of their altitude. (In competitions, all pilots must circle to the left within 5 miles of the contest site).
2. A pilot joining a thermal must not interfere or obstruct other gliders already in the thermal.
3. A pilot who is climbing quicker than other gliders must not hinder those who are being out-climbed.
4. Always try to keep yourself visible to other pilots. Avoid the other pilot's blind spots.
5. Always keep a good lookout so you know the position of other gliders at any given moment.
6. Never fly close to other gliders.

You should keep a safe distance from other gliders. Thermal flying with other gliders in a "gaggle" requires superior flying skills and an ability to think in a three dimensional way. It takes time to develop a sense where various lines of movement of other sailplanes in relation to yours will intersect in space.

When entering a thermal with another glider at approximately the same altitude, try to smoothly enter on the opposite side of the thermal, and in the same direction of travel.

Your first attempts at thermalling with other gliders should be dual with a flight instructor.

ANGLE OF BANK

In the following chart, you can see how the sink rate of the glider increases with the angle of bank. The sink rate doesn't increase dramatically until you reach a bank angle of 45 degrees or more. Also note, the diameter of a turn is substantially decreased as you increase the angle of bank. It is important to use an appropriate angle of bank for the thermal you are climbing in, but it is counter productive to attempt to circle too steeply. A common error is not banking steeply enough to remain in the thermal core.

After much experimenting, you will discover bank angles of more than 45 degrees are seldom required, and 30 degrees is the most common bank angle used by most top competition pilots. It is important to be able to perform accurate 30 degree angle of bank circles at a constant airspeed. Many pilots exaggerate the angle of bank they think they are turning. It seems like a steep turn, but in fact isn't nearly as steep as it seems. In order to fly accurate 30 degree banked turns, you should time your circles and adjust the angle of bank until you can perform a 360 degree turn in 28 seconds. A 45 degree bank angle will require 18 seconds to do 360 degrees. Once you have practiced these a few times, you will soon be able to perform these turns accurately by using the horizon and the instrument panel as a reference.

Angle of bank	Speed knots	Sink Rate knots	Load factor	Radius of turn feet	Time for 360 turn seconds
60	64	3.92	2.0	208	12.1
50	56	2.69	1.6	236	15.6
45	54	2.34	1.4	255	17.7
40	52	2.07	1.3	281	20.3
35	50	1.87	1.3	315	23.5
30	48	1.72	1.2	361	27.7
25	47	1.61	1.2	427	33.5
20	47	1.52	1.1	528	42.2
15	46	1.46	1.0	698	56.5
10	46	1.42	1.0	1040	85.0
0	45	1.39	1.0		

Circling performance of a standard
class glider at 700 lbs at sea level

A BETTER WAY TO CENTER A THERMAL

When you feel comfortable with the "fly straight for three seconds and then turn" method of centering thermals, you might try the "bank steeper in worse lift and shallow out in stronger lift" method. This requires a greater degree of piloting skill, but will get you into the best lift sooner and keep you there better.

The method is pretty much self explanatory, but suppose you are flying in a thermal giving you 5 knots lift. If the vario should begin to indicate less than 5 knots, increase the bank angle to reduce the time spent in the reduced lift. If the vario indicates better lift, reduce the bank angle (to straight and level) so you move into the stronger lift.

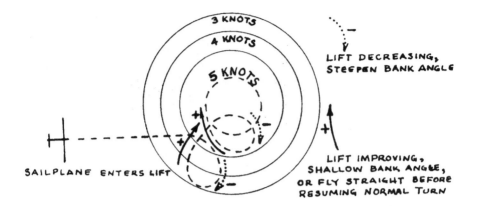

LOOK OUTSIDE

One mistake low time pilots make is not looking outside the glider most of the time. You've already learned to control airspeed by fixing a reference point on the horizon. You should have an audio variometer so you can <u>listen</u> to what the vario is indicating instead of watching the vario. While looking outside, you should be positioning yourself where the cumulus cloud looks the best, or watching other sailplane pilots and soaring birds for lift indications.

You should also be looking for the best indications of lift along your intended route as you climb in a thermal. While circling in the thermal, you will see a "picture" along your course line every 20 seconds or so as you complete each circle, making a time-lapse "movie" so you can easily discern which clouds are building, and those that have reached their mature stage and are falling apart. You should develop this skill by picking two or three clouds you might fly towards when you leave your present thermal and watching them as you complete each turn.

SET YOUR LIMIT

As a low time pilot you should set the minimum altitude you will attempt to thermal. Many serious accidents have occurred because a pilot was attempting to make a low altitude save instead of giving up and landing. Thermals are very small at low altitudes and it often isn't possible to make a save regardless of your experience or skill. As a rule of thumb, 1000 feet is a suggested minimum altitude for low time pilots. As you gain experience, you may lower this altitude, but it is rarely safe or prudent to attempt to thermal below 500 or 600 feet.

If you encounter a good thermal as you are entering your landing pattern, simply land and tell the tow pilot where to take you at a safer altitude.

CHAPTER 26

RIDGE SOARING

Few soaring pilots are fortunate to live close to a soarable ridge. Ridge soaring opens a whole new aspect to the sport of soaring. A favorable ridge makes it possible for glider pilots to fly for much longer periods of time, and provides a higher percentage of soarable days each year.

Soaring flights first began when it was discovered usable lift was to be found along a windswept ridge. The art of ridge soaring has progressed to the present day when glider pilots are making long distance, high speed flights along the Allegheny and other mountain ridges.

The ridge should be more than 200 feet high, and have a fairly steep slope. The wind direction is best when blowing at right angles to the ridge, and must blow at an angle of at least 30 degrees to the ridge. Wind speed should be no less than 10 knots. Winds above 25 knots can be uncomfortably rough.

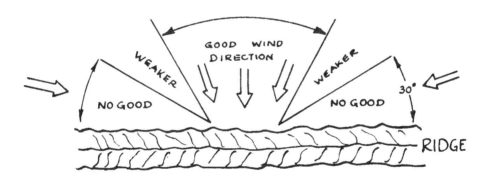

Ridge lift is in a fairly narrow zone immediately in front of the slope. Most pilots are justifiably wary about getting too close to the ridge. On the other hand, there is no ridge lift immediately above the ridge. The proper position is just in front of the ridge, and as you climb, you will need to fly further in front of the ridge. At no time should you allow yourself to drift downwind of the ridge at low altitudes. The downwind side or "leeward" side is very turbulent, and strong sinking air will be found there.

If the ridge slope is shallow, you must not allow yourself to be too low because you need to be able to glide out into the valley in case you are forced to land. Where the ridge is steep, you can be lower and/or faster since the escape route is near.

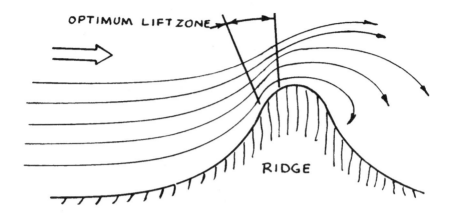

OPTIMUM LIFT ZONE

RIDGE

The airspeed you may fly will depend on several factors, such as wind direction and speed, slope height and steepness, and the kind of sailplane you are flying. You will have a choice of flying at minimum sinking speed and allowing the ridge lift to carry you as high as it can, or exchange that lifting energy into extra airspeed and fly faster, although lower. You should never permit yourself to fly at a low altitude *and* a slow airspeed. Many pilots don't understand in order to gain speed from 40 knots to 70 knots, you may lose 400 feet. If you were low and slow in ridge lift, and then ran into sinking air you had to get out of, you may not have the necessary altitude, and thus you would crash into the ridge.

There are special rules for flying in ridge lift. One of these is that you must turn away from the ridge if you make any turns. This is to keep you from running into the mountain.

If two gliders are approaching each other head on, they are both supposed to deviate their flight paths to the right to allow safe room to pass. The glider with its right wing towards the ridge may be so close it can't move to the right. Because of this, the glider with its right wing pointed towards the ridge has the right of way.

If you are the glider with your right wing pointed to the ridge and another glider is approaching head on, you will have to decide if the pilot is watching and sees you. If you have any doubt, take precautionary measures before the other glider reaches you.

Of course, if there is a lot of altitude separating the two gliders, there is less chance of a collision.

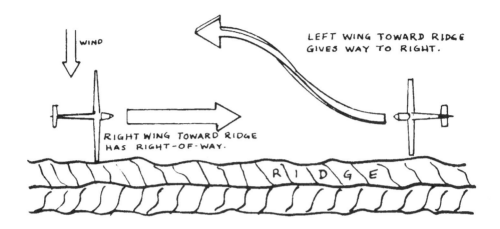

WIND

LEFT WING TOWARD RIDGE
GIVES WAY TO RIGHT.

RIGHT WING TOWARD RIDGE
HAS RIGHT-OF-WAY.

RIDGE

Never attempt to ridge soar without adequate training from an experienced instructor.

Other ridge soaring rules include:

☞ Enter ridge lift at a 45 degree angle to the ridge to avoid misjudging and colliding with the ridge.

☞ Never fly directly below or above other gliders.

☞ Overtake slower gliders by passing between the ridge and the other glider.

☞ Never fly beneath birds. They could dive through your canopy or otherwise damage your glider.

☞ Always have a field selected for a landing in case the ridge lift quits suddenly.

☞ Make all 360 degree turns well above and in front of the ridge.

☞ If you are ever forced to sink below the crest of the ridge, you should abandon all attempts at ridge soaring and move away from the ridge.

To transition from ridge lift to thermal lift from a low altitude, begin by flying figure eights in the thermal in front of the ridge, until you are high enough to safely circle.

For more detailed information about ridge soaring, I have written another book titled, *Ridge Soaring The Bald Eagle Ridge.*

CHAPTER 27

WAVE SOARING

Imagine how deep the atmosphere is. It is miles deep. Imagine all of this air being blown across a mountain or a plateau. As the air falls down the mountain, it creates a tremendous, invisible "waterfall." As air descends, it compresses and warms up. When it strikes the valley floor it compresses and the air above compresses against that air that fell before, creating a high pressure.

This compressed, warm air rises again to great heights in a series of waves, reinforced by the endless supply of air following. This is wave. It is also called "Lee Wave" or "Standing Wave." Heights exceeding 50,000 feet have been reached, and estimates are that someday, with proper life-support equipment, a glider will fly to 80,000 feet in this phenomenon.

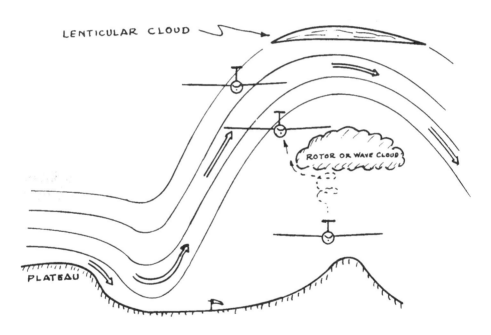

The first wave thus formed is called the "Primary Wave." The next one is called the "Secondary", and the subsequent ones are called "Tertiaries."

Underneath each wave is a zone of rolling turbulence called the "rotor." It can, on very rare occasions, be severe enough to tear an aircraft apart.

In order for wave to exist, the airflow must be rather stable. Thermal activity will often destroy the mechanism that makes wave form.

Wave conditions are often indicated by the roll cloud existing in the rotor, and a very high, smooth, lens-shaped cloud called a lenticular cloud in the wave. The roll cloud and lenticular cloud will often be long, running perpendicular to the wind direction. The lenticular cloud is constantly being formed on its upwind edge, and dissipating on its downwind edge, causing it to stand stationary, even though the air is passing through it at high speeds. The rotor cloud is often "boiling" and a strong rotation can be seen.

If the air mass is very moist, it is possible for the entire wave to fill up with cloud. A glider pilot flying high in a wave must be alert to the possibility the clear air below could fill with cloud cover, leaving the pilot above the clouds.

Wave lift is used primarily to go high, but cross country flights have been made with the notable achievements of Klaus Ohlmann in Argentina, Ray Lynskey in New Zealand, and others.

FLYING TECHNIQUE

It is possible to work your way up into the wave from ridge lift or even thermals, but most of the time, gliders are towed into the wave by a towplane. The wave area may be well marked by the roll cloud, lenticular clouds, and other gliders. Towing through the rotor can be severe, so the tow pilot will try to avoid any close contact. In some cases it is not possible to avoid the rotor. You will have to do the best you can to stay in proper tow position, but if you ever lose sight of the towplane, or get into an extreme position, you must release the tow rope.

Stay on tow until you are certain you are in wave lift. As you tow to the wave, you will most likely encounter some turbulence, but wave lift is almost always silky smooth lift. If in doubt, tow higher.

Wave lift is usually so smooth you can let go of the controls altogether for minutes at a time. It can be as smooth as siting in your living room chair.

The wind velocity is usually strong, so you must head into the wind in order not to be drifted backwards out of the lift. After you locate the wave lift, look down at the ground and determine a few references to position yourself. If you allow yourself to drift downwind out of the wave, you will encounter a very strong down current, and will lose a lot of altitude trying to penetrate forward into the lift again. If you fly too fast and penetrate forward out of the wave, it is easy to regain the lift. Simply slow down or turn slightly and drift downwind into the wave again.

The great heights attainable cause great problems as well. Special oxygen systems must be used, the gliders must be specially cared for because of the severe cold, and the human physiological factors are very important. It is beyond the scope of this book to detail the information needed to fly at the extreme altitudes possible in wave lift. When you visit a wave site, you will find textbooks written expressly about the subject, and expert instructors will guide you.

142

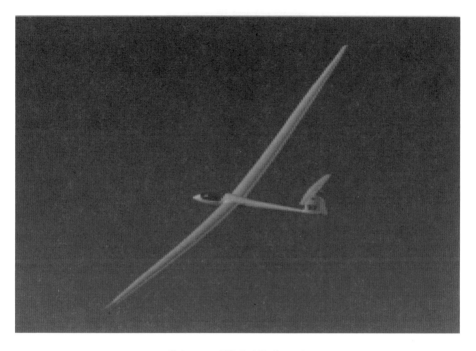

Schempp-Hirth Nimbus 4
photo by Rosalie Keene

CHAPTER 28

THE BENIGN SPIRAL MODE

Some gliders are more stable than others. Some gliders become especially stable when the dive brakes are extended.

With the dive brakes opened and your hands and feet off the controls, the glider will typically enter a slow spiral. It may oscillate a bit, the speed may vary, the bank angle may change. The glider simply descends with safe oscillations. This is the benign spiral mode, and it may save your life one day.

For instance, imagine yourself trapped on top of a solid cloud layer or perhaps suddenly engulfed in cloud. It is impossible to fly blind without visual references or special blind flying instruments and training.

Let's suppose you are flying above the clouds and the cloud layer below you closes. You know you will have to descend through the clouds.

The first step to enter the benign spiral mode is to point the glider into the wind. This has no aerodynamic purpose, but will simply allow you to perhaps come down over familiar terrain. If you were pointed downwind, you might exit the clouds many miles from where you began.

The second step is to open the dive brakes. This provides the drag necessary to cause the glider to be more stable an fly a safe speed.

Third, trim the glider for a slow speed, perhaps 45 - 50 knots.

Fourth, — and this may be the difficult part — remove your hands and feet from the controls. (Except to maintain full open dive brakes.)

During the time you are in the clouds, there will be false sensations convincing you to attempt to turn one way or another. It is very difficult to overcome the desire to manually control the glider. You must not touch the controls until you leave the cloud and have visual reference with the ground.

Obviously, the first time you try the benign spiral mode should not be the occasion of your first emergency descent. On a clear day, fly your glider to a high altitude and try the benign spiral mode while descending. After several attempts, you will gain confidence in the maneuver in case you ever need it.

WARNING: Not all sailplanes are stable in this mode. Sailplanes with all flying tails (the tailplane is one piece rather than the conventional, two piece, horizontal stabilizer and elevator.) or with flaps only for glide path control, probably will not perform a safe benign spiral. Even different sailplanes of the same type may react differently with different weights or center of gravity locations.

Try entering the benign spiral from different attitudes. From a steep turn, from a stall entry, from an incipient spin entry. Open the dive brakes, set the trim, let go of the controls and see what happens!

The glider should never increase speed beyond red line, nor slow to stall speed. If it does, the glider is not stable in the benign spiral mode.

CHAPTER 29

FLYING A SINGLE PLACE GLIDER

Sooner or later, you will satisfy the flight instructor to the point you will be allowed to fly a single-place glider. You will discover most single place gliders are more nimble, more satisfying to fly, often have better performance, and better instrumentation than the two place trainers.

Read the glider's flight manual. Find a quiet place where there are no distractions. Write down the important airspeeds, Stall speed, minimum sink speed, maximum glide speed, maneuvering speed, rough air red line, never exceed speed, and finally, the recommended pattern and landing speeds.

Pay particular attention to comments about handling characteristics, recommended stall and spin recovery procedures, any prohibited maneuvers, special preflight items, and weight and balance requirements.

Sit in the glider and get comfortable. It is important to feel right. Add any needed cushions. Adjust the seat belts and shoulder harness. Ask other people to go away for awhile so you have no distractions. Look at the instrument panel and locate each instrument. Most gliders have their own instrument panel and control layouts. Familiarize yourself with the location of the controls. You should be able to close your eyes and be able to locate any control or instrument.

Next, have an instructor who is familiar with the glider, go over any idiosyncrasies of the glider. Discuss in particular the takeoff and landing characteristics, effectiveness of the dive brakes, any pitching tendencies when the dive brakes are opened, and stalling characteristics. Ask for someone to pick up the tail to a normal gliding angle so you can get an idea where the horizon will be.

Be sure to go through the entire manufacturer's written pre-takeoff checklist which is usually located on a placard.

Many single-place gliders are pitch sensitive. To avoid pitch oscillations during the takeoff, hold the control stick slightly aft of neutral during the takeoff roll. Keep the elevator control inputs to a minimum during the initial takeoff. By holding the elevator in a position providing a positive angle of attack from the beginning of the takeoff, you will avoid unnecessary control inputs.

Take at least a 3,000 foot tow on this first flight and try to choose a soarable day, but not turbulent. Your goal should be to become as familiar with the new glider as you can before you land. A long soaring flight will help.

Investigate the glider's low speed handling characteristics, and do a few gentle stalls. A normal landing ends with slow speeds and finally the glider quits flying, so you should practice at altitude before you land. If you have the time and altitude, try turning stalls and gentle side slips.

During the landing phase, avoid the temptation of being "a little extra high". Fly the pattern just as you normally would, taking into consideration any unusual characteristics of the new glider.

CHAPTER 30

OFF-FIELD LANDINGS

Very often, people come to a gliderport and express the desire to either fly their own sailplanes cross country, or perhaps rent sailplanes for the same purpose. After talking to these pilots, it is surprising how many pilots are prepared, in their own minds, to make their first cross country attempts having not thought about the risks and ramifications of what they are about to do!

Flying cross country involves some risks. It is amazing, and even appalling how some people have made no preparation for what can be a hazardous activity! Just a brief quizzing indicates their obvious lack of knowledge and preparation.

There are several things you can do to prepare yourself for off field landings.

First, read some books. Byars and Holbrook wrote a book titled *Soaring Cross Country*; Anne Welch and Frank Irving wrote what I consider to be the one book every soaring pilot must have, titled *New Soaring Pilot*. (No longer in print.) This is a virtual encyclopedia of soaring information, especially as it applies to cross country soaring. Many pilot's have purchased Reichmann's *Soaring Cross Country*. Few pilots who own this book understand it. You should save this one until much later in your soaring career. The SSA's, *Soaring* magazine, and the British, *Sailplane and Gliding* magazine have a wealth of information including pilot reports you can learn much from. You will find stories written about first cross country attempts, and they often include some pretty scary stuff. It's a good idea to get as many back issues of these magazines as you can find.

The next thing you should do to prepare for cross country flying is to earn your SSA, ABC and Bronze badges. This is an excellent program filled with the specific skills and knowledge you should know before going cross country. The ABC badges are designed to give an orderly progression to your flight training. The Bronze badge is specifically designed towards cross country flying and off field landing skills.

The ABC and Bronze badge program is not directed by the International Gliding Commission, the international body who administers the Silver, Gold and Diamond badges. Each member country can establish it's own requirements for the ABC and Bronze badges.

If you look carefully at the requirements for the badges, you will discover a rather extensive list of things you are *supposed* to do in order to earn the badges.

Unfortunately, there is a large group of us who have been "given" the badges after fulfilling only a small portion of the requirements. For instance, the major requirement for the "A" badge is solo flight. Many pilots have soloed and been awarded the "A" badge, but if they actually look at the requirements they will discover a considerable number of items were left out of their training! Many of these same items are oriented towards successful, safe cross country flight.

So, whether you have been awarded these badges or not, inspect the actual requirements (you can find these requirements in the back of this book) and be sure you really meet all skill and knowledge requirements for every badge. Have an instructor go over those areas you know you are weak in, or you discover were omitted in your training.

One of the major requirements of the Bronze badge is more flying time, and a demonstration of your ability to stay aloft on more than one occasion.

You would agree if you are going to go cross country, you should be very familiar with the sailplane you will go in! The Bronze badge requires at least two flights of more than 2 hours duration, and 10 flights in a single place sailplane. (It's not likely you will fly cross country in a two-place glider.)

The primary goal of your first cross country flight is not whether you complete the distance, but whether you have done it safely. This boils down to whether you are able to safely land in a farmer's field if it should be necessary. Your ability to complete the task safely should not be a matter of luck. You, and your instructor, should be satisfied you are *completely* prepared for any eventuality that may occur on your first cross country flights.

The Bronze badge emphasizes accuracy landings, and tries to simulate realistic conditions. One requirement is for you to perform three solo landings into a prescribed area specified by your flight instructor. You must land and stop within a zone, usually 500 feet in length.

The requirement is for you to make three successful, successive landings from three different directions. You select a day when there is no wind, or a very light wind, and perform a left hand pattern, followed by a right hand pattern, and finally, a down wind landing. It serves no purpose to finally get three successful landings out of 25! Your skill level, before going cross country should be demonstrated by these three successful, consecutive landings, along with the other requirements of the Bronze badge.

These accuracy landings will probably be performed at your local gliderport where you have made dozens of flights. You soon learn to make your turn onto base about the old apple tree and everything comes out OK. One of the things you need to find out before making your first cross country flights is, can you perform an accurate landing at a location that doesn't have that old apple tree?

Here again, the requirements of the Bronze badge simply requires you to make two accuracy landings while accompanied by an instructor, into a strange area without the use of the altimeter. This landing should be as realistic as possible, by towing to another nearby airport where you can demonstrate your skill in a strange environment. Even better, would be a landing onto a grass runway. This will help to demonstrate to your instructor you have developed the judgment necessary to make an accurate, safe landing without the use of the altimeter.

The last requirement of the Bronze badge is to pass a written test with a passing score of at least 80%. It is a rather extensive test, and almost all the questions involve cross country knowledge. Much of the required knowledge is covered in this book, but not all of it. Your local SSA instructor will help you with this.

In flying, a 90% test result is not really satisfactory, because the 10% you don't know can hurt you. You want to know as much as possible about everything associated with making safe cross country flights. So, it is going to require some studying on your part and some intelligent realization of just what you are attempting. There **are** hazards involved here!

After you have completed the ABC and Bronze badge requirements, you are then face to face with the Silver badge.

There are three requirements for the silver badge:

1.- You must gain 1,000 meters of altitude from a previous low point,

2.- Fly for a duration of 5 hours, and

3.- Fly 50 kilometers distance.

You should perform these tasks in a safe, reasonable order. First, fly the altitude and duration requirements to prove you are able to fly high enough and long enough to fly the distance.

There is no excuse to find a person attempting a first distance flight without having demonstrated soaring abilities by being able to stay aloft more than a couple times. You should prove you can thermal and successfully stay aloft on many flights before you make a cross country attempt.

There is a natural order of progression leading to the Silver badge: First the ABC badges, followed by the Bronze badge, followed by silver altitude and duration, followed finally by the distance.

SILVER DISTANCE

Before you consider the Silver distance flight, have a serious talk with an experienced flight instructor. Find out if the instructor feels you are exhibiting the skills to safely go cross country. Don't make this decision on your own. Often, our desires get far ahead of our abilities.

150

Certainly, we all want to proceed with the Gold, Diamond, and 1,000 km awards. I hope you eventually fly in soaring contests, and set records. But sometimes we are blind to the real facts as they apply to our own abilities. An experienced flight instructor can be an excellent guide as to whether you are truly ready for that first cross country flight.

Remember this also: It matters little to anybody else if you fly cross country or earn any badges.

Our accomplishments become very personal in nature. You can no longer impress anyone with a diamond badge. Most of the very experienced pilots don't even wear them.

You won't impress many people with a Diamond badge, but if you have an accident while attempting a cross country flight, you will lose the respect of most other soaring pilots. If you go cross country, and have an accident, or incident because of your lack of skill, preparation, or maturity, it will reflect on you for the rest of your flying career. There are many people who used to fly gliders, but no longer are involved in the sport because of the loss of respect among their peers.

Accidents can happen to anyone, no matter their skill level or training. However, do your best to make complete preparations before you fly cross country.

OFF FIELD LANDINGS

One of the things you might be able to do to prepare for cross country and off field landings is to take an off field landing course using a motor glider. We take the motorglider and fly a 150 km triangle course the pilot has planned. During the flight you will make about 10 simulated off-field landings as well as navigation skills.

Before the flight, you will discuss the flight plan, review map reading and navigation. The entire course, including preflight and post flight briefings takes about 3 hours. The flight begins with off field landings into easy areas.

The pilot climbs to about 2,000 feet above ground (the altimeter is covered) and then begins a glide in the direction of the first turn point with the engine at idle. The motor glider glides lower and the pilot selects a suitable landing area and enters the landing pattern. If everything goes well, the instructor allows the glide to continue until it is obvious what the outcome would have been, then accelerates the engine and begins another climb to about 2,000 feet. During the climb, the instructor reviews the student's performance on the landing attempt.

Several landing attempts are made on the way to the first turn point, then the student flies toward the second turn point. The second leg is used to teach navigation skills as well as identifying suitable landing areas. After the second turn point is reached, the student navigates along the final leg until it is obvious the home gliderport will be found. More off field landings are performed into more difficult areas.

Ten off field landings during one flight is probably more off field landings than the average pilot will perform in several years of active flying. This is a quick way to develop the learning curve and discover weaknesses and strengths.

The typical glider pilot learns off field landings quite differently. Even if the pilot doesn't have an accident, there is no one to critique the performance and suggest different or better ways to handle each situation. I remember my first off field landing very well. Things went well, and I don't remember any mistakes. But, if it were a flight instructor standing in the alfalfa field instead of a farmer, he might have made several suggestions. Perhaps there was a better field nearby. Perhaps I flew my downwind leg a bit too close or far away. Maybe my turns were not entirely correct, or the airspeed wasn't what it should be. The benefits I could have derived if a flight instructor were with me would have been very valuable.

It was more than a year before I made another off field landing. It was five years before I made ten off field landings. It takes a glider pilot a long time to make enough off field landings to understand, and know how to do it.

Last year, I did 400 off field landings with students in a motor glider. *With few exceptions, each one of those pilots would have crashed during one of their first attempts at a real landing.* (Remember we begin with easy fields.)

During the 1987 Sports Class Nationals, more than 30% of the pilots entered in the contest damaged their ships during off field landings!

The reason for the high accident rate is lack of education, and preparation for off field landings. Incorrect, incomplete flight training probably plays a role too.

The off field landing course using a motor glider is an excellent way to teach pilots to be safer.

FIELD SELECTION

OK, let's look at some of the factors involved with off field landings and see what kinds of information you need to consider.

SIZE

The first consideration is the size of the field itself. The typical farmers field is more than big enough. Farmers don't cultivate very small fields because they can't get their equipment into it, and it is not economical to grow crops in tiny fields. Oh sure, there are exceptions, but by and large, there are lots of fields big enough. New England probably has more small fields than other parts of the country.

While planning your first flight, consider which area will give you the best opportunity for large, easy landing areas. Ask other experienced pilots for their help in choosing a reasonable task. In many parts of the country you can fly many miles and always be in range of an airport.

How large a field do we need? Even small fields are seldom less than 1500 feet in length. Mid-west and southern fields are often larger, sometimes reaching a mile square. There are far fewer tiny farm fields than there are large fields.

A glider rolls less than 500 feet on level ground during a normal landing, so the typical farmers field is normally plenty big enough. As you look down from several thousand feet you will see lots of large fields

COLOR

The next obvious difference as you look at the fields is color. There are pretty green fields, and brown fields, and yellow fields. Each color indicates a different crop or landing surface. When I asked one pilot what color would indicate the best surface, he said "Black with a white stripe down the middle." Well, it is unlikely we will find a runway every time we need one, so what is the next best color?

We know farmers only cultivate the best fields. Over decades of time, the farmer has picked out the big rocks. Especially poor fields are left for pasture land. These fields have rocks that would damage farm equipment, or have too steep a slope. Those fields usually look rough even from the air. Fields used for grazing animals are usually not a good choice for off field landings.

What does cultivated mean? In the recent past, we have had textbooks suggest plowed fields make excellent landing areas. Not so! Stop by a farm field being plowed. The tractor plows the earth into giant rolls of deep-turned dirt. There are huge rolls and clods of earth. Certainly a place you would never want to land a glider.

A cultivated field has been plowed, harrowed, raked, smoothed, and probably planted with a crop. The dirt even looks soft, sometimes fluffy. A landing in this type of surface is almost impossible to damage the glider. A popular saying is "You won't get hurt if you land in dirt!"

The color of dirt around the country can be red, tan or black, but the most common color is brown. The best color for an off field landing field is earth color. The earth color indicates the probability of a freshly cultivated field.

A cultivated field will probably have seeds planted and the seeds may have germinated and begun to grow. As the plants begin to grow, the brown field will begin to change color beginning with a light green tint until it becomes a full grown, lush green. The emerald green color of a full grown crop is definitely a color to stay away from. Some crops are yellow as they mature, such as sunflowers. Some crops become dirt brown color and from a distance look like a freshly cultivated field. You have to be aware of these, especially in the fall when the farmers are cultivating for winter wheat. Corn must dry thoroughly before the farmers put it into storage. If the corn contains excess moisture, it will rot in the silos. Dry corn stalks look just like a freshly cultivated field from a distance.

After a crop matures, the farmer harvests the crop. Most of the time the crop is cut close to the ground. The lush green of a mature crop becomes a yellow-green color after it is cut. A freshly mown field is an inviting place to land. What is the difference between a field that has been recently cultivated and one that has just recently been harvested?

The answer is time. Three months have gone by from the time the field was planted and the time it is harvested. During this time, animals have come in and built their underground homes. The holes they dig are difficult to see, just about landing gear size, and can cause considerable damage to the glider. Also, some farmers lay irrigation pipes through the fields and cut off the crop above the pipes leaving them hidden. A recently harvested crop can hide some very serious hidden hazards.

Later in the year you will find the farmers harvesting some crops and planting new crops so you have a selection of fields to choose from. During mid to late summer, the fields are mostly growing crops and recently harvested crops, so you may not have freshly cultivated fields to choose from. In this case, a recently harvested field may be the best choice. Be aware there are serious hazards in these fields.

One of the interesting things we do with the motor glider is to fly over a recently harvested field and spot animal holes. They are easy to see from altitude, but as you fly the pattern and line up on final approach, the holes disappear, hidden by the short stubble.

Earth color is the best color, the second best color is the light green color of a short crop, and then the yellow-green of a recently harvested crop. A dark, lush emerald green crop is probably too deep to safely land in. Here in our local area, the farmers have a saying, *"knee high by the fourth of July"*, which means the corn crop will be a good one if it gets that high by that time. For glider pilots here in the northeastern USA, it means you can't land in corn after the fourth of July. The farmers in your area probably have other rules of thumb which are useful to you.

The color of a field should be uniform. If there are light and dark spots in the field, it indicates the field is not level. The low spots will collect moisture and the crop grows better. Also, dark and light brown colors indicate where the moisture has caused the dirt to look wet, which indicates low spots. Drainage ditches usually show up as dark brown or greener areas.

Farm equipment can't mow very close to fence rows, and leave a dark green stripe along the fence.

OBSTRUCTIONS

We have listed several factors so far, and we will discuss more. It is impossible to list these factors in the order of importance because each of them are equally important. If I had to choose one factor above all, however, I would choose obstructions as the number one important consideration when choosing an off field landing field. This is also one of the factors few glider pilots know to consider, and one of the chief factors when analyzing off field landing accidents.

An obstruction has the effect of 10 times it's height. If you fly over a 100 foot tree at the end of the field, it will reduce the effective length of that field by 1,000 feet. During the motorglider off field landing course, we choose a field that is very long, say 3,000 feet with a tall obstruction at one end. The pilot approaches the field and notes where the glider would have touched down. We climb up and look down to see just how we would have done, and it is quite impressive to see the great distance we covered because of the obstruction.

We then go to another field with no obstructions. This field is just 500 feet long. The approach continues and it is obvious how easy it is to land in such a short field when there is no obstruction.

The reason an obstruction has such a big effect is we must clear the obstruction by a safe margin, and we will tend to clear it by even more than necessary.

We also must clear with a safe margin of speed, probably will use more speed than necessary. As soon as we clear the obstruction, we will encounter calmer air, which will allow the glider to float further along. The combined effect is the obstruction affects us more than we would expect.

Every field has one kind of obstruction; a fence. You can assume every field has a fence around it. In addition to fences, there may be electric wires, and telephone wires. You cannot see wires. But you can usually see the poles, and even the shadows the poles make. Later in the afternoon when you probably will be landing, the shadows may be very long and easy to see.

Every structure, no matter how small will probably have a wire running to it; perhaps strung between trees. Every road, even a dirt road or path will have power lines along it.

Power lines and wires are my biggest concern when landing off field.

If you don't learn anything else, remember to avoid obstructions!

SLOPE

Every glider pilot seems to know you must land uphill regardless of the wind direction. Slope you can discern from the air is much steeper than it appears. Landing uphill turns out to be really OK. The roll-out is very short. The glider stops quickly, even when landing down wind, so there is less chance for damage by running over or through something. If the slope is too steep, you have the risk of the glider rolling backwards after you stop.

If you discern slope or undulations from the air, the slope is much worse than it appears from the air.

When landing uphill, be sure to use extra airspeed to lift the nose of the glider higher than normal, and expect the glider to reduce airspeed much quicker than a level field landing. Also, there is an optical illusion when landing uphill which may cause you to land short of your intended touch down spot, so pick a spot well into the field.

WHICH FIELD?

Given several choices, which field do you choose? Some pilots develop a mind set about certain criteria. Since earth color is the best color, they only look at brown fields. Or, they may only choose large fields, or ones without obstructions. You must learn to look for all these features and pick the field with the best overall qualities.

There may be a brown field, a light green field, and a yellow-green field. The brown field is very short. The light green field has a mottled, uneven color. The yellow-green field is very long with high obstructions. Knowing nothing else, the best choice is probably the yellow-green field.

I have made hundreds of off field landings without even a minor scratch on the glider. An off field landing can be just as normal as an on airport landing. With one exception, and that is wires. I look <u>very</u> close for wires!

WHERE NOT TO LAND

School yards and playgrounds have many hidden hazards, but more important, landings here cause the local citizens to be concerned about their children's safety, even if there were no children using the playground at the time.

Golfers see no humor in a glider sitting on a fairway.

Many crops are very valuable, such as tobacco, or are planted on top of mounds of dirt, such as cotton, or are irrigated by low ditches or hillocks, especially in dry climates.

You may be forced to land in these areas, but be forewarned that you may be in for an unpleasant experience.

Fields near gliderports hosting frequent glider contests usually have farmers who have had their crop damaged by some unthinking, uncaring, inconsiderate, glider pilot and/or crew. You can expect to be met by an irate farmer who justifiably intends to get even with the next glider pilot.

WHAT TO DO WHEN CONFRONTED BY AN IRATE FARMER

First, make it your every intention to try to change this farmer's image of some members of the soaring community by seeking him or her out before he finds out from someone else a glider has landed in his fields.

156

Show a sincere concern for the property and crop, and offer right away to pay for any damage, no matter how small. Be nice to the kids, and wife. Take pictures of the kids sitting in the glider, and send them to the farmer so they will remember this exciting event the rest of their lives.

Show the farmer how you will remove the glider with the least possible additional damage. Show how little damage you have done during the landing. Show your appreciation to the lucky circumstances that may have saved your life or certain damage to the glider had you not found this excellent field. Admire the tractor, and the modern equipment or how healthy the cows look.

Sooner or later, it will happen. You will find the world's roughest, toughest most unreasonable farmer. He will most likely threaten that he will not allow you to remove the glider. He may even want to call the police. The police are your best ally. The sooner they are called, the better.

Politely offer to make the phone call to show your willingness to use an impartial arbitrator.

Inform the farmer the glider is covered with insurance and any claim will be covered by the insurance company. Take the obvious information needed by the insurance company. In the presence of the police officer, inform the farmer if you are forced to leave the glider sit in the field, you will unwillingly do so, because you have no choice. However, the glider then becomes the responsibility of the farmer to protect from any damage, for which the insurance company will sue for. The police officer will see the reasoning of this final ploy and convince the farmer you are right, and the farmer will most likely reluctantly allow you to take your glider.

You should still take the pictures of the kids.

At Christmas time, send the farmer a copy of the SSA calendar. It is an inexpensive way to say thank you.

DECISION HEIGHTS

There are certain important decision heights you must use while flying cross country:

First, never consider flying cross country with less than 3,000 feet above ground cloud base. If you can't get to 3,000 feet, the chances of an off field landing increase dramatically. In fact, most glider sites have soaring conditions much better than this during much of the year, and you should choose a day with 5,000 to 6,000 foot cloud bases for your first cross country flights.

While flying cross country, as you descend to 3,000 feet above the ground, fly towards an area with the best possible landing fields.

When you descend to 2,000 feet, select several possible landing fields and search for thermals within easy reach of these fields.

When you are 1,200 to 1,500 feet above the ground, you should be entering the upwind leg of a specific landing field with an alternate field within easy reach in case you discover a hazard with the primary field.

THE LANDING PATTERN

A landing pattern should have four legs: an upwind leg; a crosswind leg; a downwind leg; a base leg and the final approach. These legs form a rectangle around the landing area whether it's an airport or a farmer's field. Every time you make a landing at the home airport, practice these rectangular landing patterns, so when you make an off field landing, you will have a better chance to make a satisfactory landing pattern.

At 1,000 feet you should be on the upwind leg of your chosen field so you can fly the rectangular pattern. You will look for hidden obstructions, slope, animals, and the crop as you fly around it. You should be able to tell the wind direction by the drift as you fly the pattern.

It may not be possible to fly entirely around the field. You may have misjudged the height, and may be lower than you thought. When landing off-field, you must expect to have some difficulty in judging the exact height above the ground. As you fly around the pattern, pay particular attention to visual clues that will help you judge height, and be prepared to alter the pattern so you can reach a reasonable height along the downwind leg. It is often necessary to cut the corners from the rectangular pattern and even cut across the chosen field at midpoint to arrive at a safe height on the downwind leg.

When you are on the downwind leg, opposite the intended touch down point, you should be about 500 feet high. At 500 feet, you have the use of all your judgmental faculties: sizes of familiar objects, angles, and depth perception. Depth perception only becomes accurate in judging distances and height within 500 feet. This height will have to be adjusted higher if you are encountering, or expect to encounter winds or turbulence.

Remember, the altimeter is the least reliable instrument in the glider. You must develop the skill necessary to judge heights without the altimeter.

You can often judge height very accurately using the 45 degree method. Pick a point on the ground that is a 45 degree angle from your location. Then judge how far this point is from a point directly under the glider. Your height is equal to this distance.

Line A is equal to line B

ALTERNATE FIELDS

When selecting an area for possible landing fields, try to choose an area with several optional fields. When you narrow your selection to one or two, consider what you would do if you suddenly noticed some hazard making the primary field undesirable.

It is not always possible to have an alternate field, but in many, if not most, cases there is some alternate place to land. While carefully inspecting the primary field, keep in mind the alternate, and try to inspect it too.

If the primary field turns out to have a hazard, you must not place yourself into the situation of quickly turning to another field with an even more serious hazard! You selected the primary field over others, so the other fields nearby must have had some features you did not like. It is often better to deal with a known hazard rather than suddenly changing to a different field and finding an even worse situation. Last minute maneuvering to align yourself with an alternate field may place you into severe risk if you must maneuver the sailplane in a hazardous manner, or maneuver beyond your skill level.

It is often better to deal with a known hazard rather than suddenly changing to a different field and finding an even worse situation.

Another interesting situation seems to occur when pilots are confronted with many good landing areas. Some pilots never seem to make an absolute decision when faced with this "problem", and end up very low, with no chance to fly a proper, well planned landing.

Most of us normally fly a left hand landing pattern at our home airports. When you make an off field landing, it should also be a left hand pattern. Do what you are most familiar with! If you normally fly a right hand pattern, try to do a right hand pattern when you land off field. Its not always possible, but keep this in mind.

PATTERN AIRSPEED

The pattern speed should be the same as if you were landing in the same conditions at your home airfield. During this whole landing pattern you want to keep things as normal as possible. The best speed to fly is best glide speed, plus 1/2 any wind, plus a factor if it is turbulent. You will tend to fly faster than normal during an off field landing.

THE DOWNWIND LEG

When we are under stress, we want to be close to whatever represents security. During an off field landing, the security is the field itself. Most pilots will fly very much closer to the landing field when they make an off field landing or when landing at an unfamiliar airport.

If you fly too close to the field during the downwind leg, you will not be able to have a reasonable length base leg, and only have room for a 180 degree turn. The base leg is probably the most important of all the legs, when trying to make an accurate landing. A proper base leg will allow you to make adjustments by using the spoilers and/or turning slightly away from or towards the field to help adjust for height. While flying on the downwind leg, keep a distance that allows you to be at least 45 degree to the field, and better yet 30 degrees. The important thing, is not the angle you are from the field, but the understanding that being too close makes it impossible to have a reasonable length base leg.

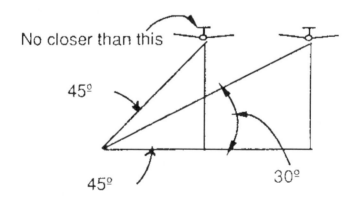

No closer than this

45°

45°   30°

THE TURN ONTO BASE LEG

Probably the single, most common error made by pilots is turning onto base leg too early. This places them in an awkward position of being higher than they should be. They are forced to use full spoilers, and perhaps even a sideslip to get the glider down. In many cases, they are so high, a normal landing cannot be made at the intended point and they are forced into the situation of landing further into the field. Some pilots are so high they are tempted to try a very dangerous 360 degree turn to lose height.

We are all basically conservative people, and we realize that without an engine, we don't want to go so far along the downwind leg we cannot make it back to the field. Many of us will overcompensate by turning onto the base leg too early, and then have difficulty making the glider descend steep enough to land at the intended point.

TURNS

During an off field landing, there is a lot going on, and you will be under great stress. There are a lot of things you are watching for. However, when you make the turns onto base and final; during that brief five seconds or so that it takes to make each turn, *there is nothing more important than keeping the yaw string absolutely straight*!

Our primary problem in glider safety is the stall-spin from a turn at low altitude. If you keep the yaw string straight, and the nose of the glider below the horizon in a normal gliding attitude, it is impossible to stall, or spin during these turns in the landing pattern.

WHERE TO LAND

As a beginning cross country pilot, you should land in the middle of the biggest suitable field available. A more experienced pilot may choose to land closer to a gate to make the retrieve easier. However, a new, inexperienced pilot may roll *through* the gate! A new pilot should be thinking about the safest, surest plan of action. Take no risks. A little inconvenience retrieving from the middle of a big field is nothing compared to the inconvenience of waiting months during the best part of a soaring season while waiting to have the glider repaired!

You folks out west have to use some common sense when you apply this last rule. Some of those fields are a mile square, and to land in the middle of them may be a long way to the access gate!

TOUCHDOWN

You want to land with the least amount of energy so the glider rolls the shortest distance. Rolling even a couple inches further than necessary may mean dropping into a hole, or hitting a rock that may damage the glider. A proper off field touch down speed is as slow as possible. This means a tail low, very slow speed landing. The very best, and safest attitude at touch down may be a tail first landing. When you are landing the glider on a day to day basis at your home gliderport, you should practice this type of landing <u>every time</u>. Watch the expert pilots and you will discover the best pilots land this way every time. It is the low time rookie pilots who land fast with the tail up in the air, and the nose close to the ground. Inspect the belly of a glider and you can tell what kind of pilot flies it!

Avoid the temptation to allow the glider to roll closer to the gate. Sooner or later you will roll over a rock or into a hole.

LIVESTOCK

Sheep are a hazard: They panic and run and bounce around all excited. You may land in a large field with sheep on one side, and decide to land on the other side. The sheep will see you and suddenly be everywhere!

Cattle are curious creatures (so are we). There are lots of stories about cattle, but I remember once in Texas when I landed three fields away from a rather large herd of cattle. I walked to the ranchers house to make the phone call back to the crew, and then returned to the glider. It was surrounded by hundreds of cattle! They looked and licked, but didn't damage anything. Sometimes it is useful to raise a commotion away from the glider to attract the cows attention away from the glider.

Horses are very often very valuable creatures and may become excited and run, injuring themselves. Horse owners often become excited and run around and may injure you!

Finally, if you see a single cow in a field, it is probably an angry bull!

CHAPTER 31

EMERGENCY PROCEDURES

CANOPY OPENS ON TOW

Handled properly, this emergency should end up being nothing more than an embarrassment. Unfortunately, deaths have occurred simply because the pilot forgot to properly close and lock the canopy before commencing the launch, then mishandled the emergency.

A properly performed pre-takeoff checklist is important. Most of us use an acronym to remember the checklist items. CB-SI(F)T-CBE, (the "E" stands for Emergency plan) or the less popular ABCCCDE series of letters help us remember those items recognized as important.

Older sailplanes were not required to have a written pre-takeoff checklist in the cockpit. The pilot was expected to use a memorized one. Modern sailplane manufacturers must supply a written pre-takeoff checklist which is displayed in the cockpit. This checklist may, or may not, include all the items in the memorized checklist. For this reason, it is necessary for each pilot to be familiar with the memorized checklist and review it also before each takeoff.

The aircraft may have some peculiar item that must be checked before each flight. This item may not be included in the standard, memorized acronym. For this reason, the written checklist provided by the manufacturer takes precedence. The pilot must be sure to perform the written checklist.

It is common practice to perform the mandatory written checklist followed by the memorized one. During the second check, the pilot is not required to redo those things done in the written checklist. Simply be positive all items in each checklist are performed.

If the pilot fails to perform any of the items, it is very possible a serious situation can occur which can lead to an accident or even death.

Almost every experienced pilot has forgotten to perform some item in the checklist. Pilots with extensive experience have probably forgotten almost every item in the checklist at least once. It is almost always a matter of being in a hurry, or being distracted by some outside influence that causes this lapse in what we all know is a serious procedure.

It is important for each of us to know and understand the importance of a properly performed pre-takeoff checklist, to use procedures that ensure completion of the entire checklist, and to avoid interruptions.

Allow enough time to perform the checklist. Take your time while performing the checklist. Do not hurry. If there are reasons for you to hurry, stop the launching sequence, get out of the glider if necessary, and allow the reason for haste to pass before beginning the launch sequence again.

Never allow anyone to disrupt your train of thought as you perform this critically important checklist. If you are disrupted, consider beginning the checklist again, rather than commencing from the middle of the checklist.

OK, despite all of the above, you are taking off, and the canopy begins to open. In many cases, you will have some warning. The canopy begins to move, or there may be extra air noise. If the ground is rough, the canopy may make a bumping noise.

If the glider is still on the ground, or possibly just airborne, consider aborting the tow, and land straight ahead. It is far better to admit the mistake and suffer a bit of embarrassment than to continue the flight and possibly lose the canopy.

If the glider is airborne, and you detect the canopy is unlatched and beginning to open, press on the rudder that causes a slight side slip in the direction that would cause the airflow to keep the canopy closed. This requires some thinking before the emergency happens. Right now, as you read this article, think about the glider you fly. Which side does the canopy hinge? Most European gliders hinge on the right side, so the pilot would press on the left rudder to cause the airflow to keep the canopy from flying open.

It doesn't take much rudder pressure to keep the canopy closed. There is no need for a severe side slip.

If you fly a glider that has a front hinging canopy, it is unlikely that anything will happen if the canopy is left unlocked, other than an increased amount of air noise. The airflow will keep the canopy most of the way down. It may bump up and down slightly, and cause a distraction, but the glider flies well in this condition. It may not be possible to close and lock the canopy while airborne, so you must land to get it secure.

If the glider you are flying has a rear hinged canopy like a Jantar, there may be little warning before the canopy is gone.

After applying the slight side slip, pause a moment to assess the situation. Make a conscious effort to not make a hasty decision. Your brain will have you try something quickly, but not necessarily the correct thing.

After a brief pause, you may be able to use one hand to hold the canopy closed while you continue the aero tow. Avoid the temptation to abort the tow at a low altitude just because you are having an emergency. It is probably better to continue the tow to a normal height, and then deal with the emergency.

It is possible the airflow causes enough suction that you won't be able to close and latch the canopy with one hand during the tow. After you release, you can slow down and then try to lock the canopy. If the air is turbulent, it may be difficult to fly with one hand, hold the canopy closed with the other, and also find some way to operate the release. It may be necessary to tow to a higher than normal height to reach calm air before releasing.

If the canopy opens all the way during the tow, it may happen suddenly. Your instinctive reaction of reaching for the canopy will probably be incorrect.

If the canopy suddenly opens all the way, it may break, or come off, or both. Canopies are expensive, but have no value compared to human life. Your first and only responsibility is to fly the glider. Maintain control. Maintain correct position with the towplane. As in most emergencies, pause a moment to assess the situation before responding to a knee-jerk reaction. (Where do you think the word "jerk" came from? Maybe from Samuel Jerk who reacted improperly to a simple emergency and caused a serious accident!)

Again, if the canopy opens all the way, and either comes off, or simply hangs to the side of the glider, it is probably better to take a normal height tow to allow time for you to calm down, and then perform a landing.

If the canopy is hanging open against the side of the aircraft, it is unlikely you will be able to close it. Leave it open. The glider will continue to fly well.

There may be a lot of wind blowing against your face. Your hat will blow off. Maybe your sunglasses too. It may help to duck down a bit to avoid the direct airflow. You may use your one hand to shield your eyes from the airflow, too.

If you have the presence of mind, and the time, inform the folks on the gliderport by radio that you have an emergency, and will be landing soon.

Here's a first hand account by someone who experienced this problem:

I had a canopy open in flight some time ago. I was giving spin training in a two place Lark. It is difficult to see if the Lark's canopy is correctly latched. This time it wasn't. The takeoff and tow were normal. After a few clearing turns, we entered a spin. The instant the spin began, bang! The canopy flew open.

Miraculously, it didn't break, but broke the restraining cable, thoroughly jamming fully 180 degrees from its normally closed position. The frame twisted and distorted slightly, the leading edge of the wing was dinged. The spin, the noise of the canopy frame slamming and scraping against the wing, and the sudden rush of air were pretty disorienting.

Fortunately, we had plenty of altitude. After the initial shock passed and I realized what had happened, and there was no other damage, I relaxed a little.

I noticed no difference in handling characteristics. We ultimately made a normal landing. The only damage was the dented wing, the distorted canopy frame and two sets of underwear.

Here are the lessons learned. Always wear sunglasses with cable earpieces or those straps that connect the earpieces behind your head. The wind force was very strong. I'm glad I was in the back seat and had a student to partially block the wind flow. Even though my sunglasses did not come off, my eyes watered profusely after a few seconds. It was very hard to see.

Turning your head even a little lets the air flow around the glasses, making things much worse. I was constantly trying to find a wind shielded position where I could dry my eyes.

Communication with my passenger was also impossible. The wind noise was just too loud.

Open canopies are spectacular, but not, in themselves, particularly dangerous. The moral: be calm, stay cool, don't panic and continue to fly the glider.

Bob Greenblatt

DOWN WIND LANDINGS

There are three principal hazards involved with down wind landings.

First, there is the illusion of excess speed as you get closer tot he ground.

Normal landings are made into the wind. Your airspeed indicator may typically read 55 knots on final approach, however, the actual ground speed is almost always less because of the normal headwind. The ground goes by slowly on hundreds of normal landings you make. With a tailwind, the wind speed is added to the indicated airspeed. The resulting ground speed is very much faster, which makes the pilot think the airspeed is faster than normal.

Headwind	Tailwind
Indicated approach speed 55 knots	Indicated approach speed 55 knots
Head wind - 10 knots	Tail wind + 10 knots
Ground Speed 45 knots	Ground speed 65 knots

Note the difference in apparent speed is 20 knots faster with a tailwind.

There is a temptation to try to make the glider slow down to what "looks" normal. If you are distracted by what is going on, (very likely) you may inadvertently slow the glider to stall speed. As the stall occurs, your brain becomes overloaded, and it is unlikely you will react correctly. The result, of course is a crash.

166

To over come this hazard, you should develop the habit of monitoring the airspeed indicator every few seconds during the landing phase of every landing, and increase this monitoring whenever you realize you are making a downwind landing.

To monitor the airspeed indicator is not the same as constantly looking at it. If you blink your eyes for the briefest possible time, you will discover your brain retains the image long enough to "read" the indicator.

This is an important skill to develop. You can practice as you drive a car. Try blinking on the speedometer as you drive along the highway, and you will see what I mean. By the way, this is much easier with an analog display than a digital display.

The second hazard is the possibility you may not be able to get the glider onto the ground before running out of runway, or farmer's field. The glider goes a lot further with a tailwind.

Many pilots incorrectly turn onto the base leg of a normal, into the wind landing, so close to the runway and so high they must use most, if not all of the dive brakes and/or flaps to get the glider down to the intended spot. The result is a steep approach.

If these same pilots make the turn onto base leg or final before they realize they are landing downwind, they may be attempt some unusual and dangerous maneuvering to keep from overshooting the landing area. Many off field landing accidents occur in this manner.

Below a few hundred feet, any abrupt, unplanned maneuvering is exceedingly dangerous.

To avoid this hazard, review your normal, into the wind landing practices and determine if your normal landings require full dive brake usage for any but brief periods. If you find you are using full dive brakes or flaps during your normal landings, you are probably using a too steep approach angle as your normal approach.

If you perceive you are making a down wind landing, extend the downwind leg much further than normal.

The third hazard is the eventual uncontrollability of the glider during the ground roll.

The glider's control surfaces must have air moving over them to work. Once the airflow reduces to some minimum rate, they no longer work at all. The ailerons will typically lose effectiveness before the rudder.

We use the rudder to steer the glider once we are on the ground. We keep the wings level, or one wing slightly low in a cross wind, as we roll along the ground to a stop. The ailerons and rudder are effective to a very slow airspeed, however, if we are making a downwind landing, the glider will finally slow to the point there is not enough air moving over the control surfaces for them to be effective.

If you have a 10 knot tail wind, the glider may be moving along the ground at 15 or 20 miles per hour when the controls finally lose their effectiveness. The pilot is now a passenger in an unguided missile!

You may have heard, or read about control reversal in these circumstances. The theory is that at very slow speeds and a tail wind, you should push on the right rudder pedal to turn left. The theory is correct, but it doesn't work in practice. (This control reversal effect is important while taxiing some power planes with a tail wind.)

As you roll along the ground, and the glider begins to turn a wrong direction, how is the pilot supposed to know if control reversal has begun? If you move the controls in a normal manner, and the glider doesn't respond, I suppose you could try the opposite direction, however, you have just made matters worse, and the time from control reversal to a full stop in a glider is very short indeed.

The important thing you must realize is that on every down wind landing, the controls are going to lose their effectiveness during the last part of the roll-out. You should take this into consideration by pointing the glider into an open area while you have positive control, and keep the glider going straight. Never plan to make a turn at the end of the roll out.

Never aim the glider towards any object, or attempt to stop the glider near other gliders, or people.

Be prepared for the eventual loss of control and, when you perceive it happening, apply the wheel brake and stop the glider as soon as possible.

INTENTIONAL GROUNDLOOP

If you perceive the landing area is small, and a groundloop may be necessary, line up the final approach along the downwind edge of the landing area to allow adequate room to perform the groundloop. A groundloop is best performed by turning into any crosswind that may be present. (See drawing next page.)

There is a potential risk in attempting to groundloop a glider. If the glider is still travelling fast at the beginning of the groundloop, the outboard wing may be traveling so fast through the air it may generate enough lift to cause the glider to begin to roll, which could cause it to become inverted!

The possible scenario would have the glider pilot realizing the glider may not stop before striking an object at the end of the landing area, and the pilot may attempt to begin an intentional groundloop while the glider is still airborne and still moving fast. Placing one wing on the ground and pressing the complementary rudder will cause the glider to yaw quickly, swerve, and turn, however, it is also possible to cause the unwanted rolling motion.

168

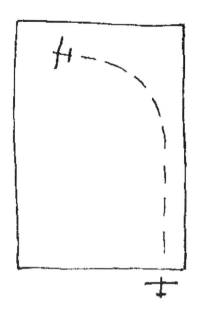

To perform a safer groundloop, it is important to start the groundloop with a minimum amount of energy. The glider should be on the ground, and allowed to roll towards the hazardous object before beginning the groundloop. Maximum braking, including pressing the nose of the glider against the ground should be attempted in an effort to slow the glider as much as possible.

Besides the risk of the glider becoming inverted, there is the less life threatening risk of breaking the glider in half or other damage during a groundloop. The less energy at the beginning of the groundloop, the less likely there will be damage.

After slowing the glider as much as possible, press the upwind wing to the ground with aileron pressure, and apply the rudder in the same direction. Continue applying the wheel brake, and press fully forward on the control stick. This keeps the tail in the air longer, helping to prevent the tail from breaking off, and keeps the wing at the lowest angle of attack to help prevent the outboard wing from generating too much lift.

After a groundloop, or any harsh maneuver, the glider must be closely inspected for possible damage. When disassembling the glider, pay close attention to any unusual effort to remove the wing pin(s), wings, and tailplane. An experienced mechanic will not only look at the obvious places, but also the areas stresses might have traveled to. For instance, a groundloop with a T-tailed glider might cause over-stressing at the base of the vertical stabilizer, and/or fuselage because of the twisting loads caused by the mass of the tailplane being on top of the fin. The pilot may not be the best person to inspect the glider, because of the desire not to find any damage. Damage is often found months after miss-use of the aircraft.

WATER LANDING

OK, you are flying over the Amazon jungle having completely overflown your intended goal of Miami Florida. (The flight began in central Pennsylvania, but Miami was fogged in, so you continued over the Gulf of Mexico on the front side of a hurricane.) You are getting low, with dense forest everywhere. The only possible landing is a large lake, roughly 1,000 feet in diameter. Where should you plan to land the glider?

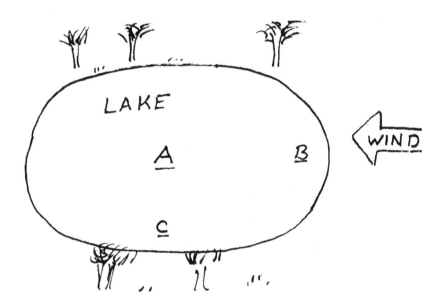

The choices are:

A. In the middle of the lake.
B. Touch down just short of the shore and allow the glider to slide up onto the beach.
C. Parallel to the shoreline.

Landing in the middle of the lake will require a long swim to shore. If you don't drown, the crocodiles will eat you.

Touching down just short of the shoreline and sliding up onto the beach, sounds good, but what if you misjudge? This isn't something we practice, and landing on water, especially if it is smooth, can be very tricky. You just might bounce off the water and into the trees, or touch down and stop very far from shore.

The safest approach is to plan the final approach parallel to the shoreline near the beach. The glider touches down and comes to rest near the shore where you can swim, or even walk to shore.

Should the landing gear be up or down?

170

One hazard exists with some gliders (perhaps many designs).

The ASW-20C owners manual has the following statement:

(4) Emergency landings on water :

Using a glider with a fuselage of similar shape to that of the ASW-20C, a water landing was attempted with the landing gear retracted. This showed that the fuselage does not "water ski", but the entire cockpit is forced under water. In depths less than two meters the pilot is in utmost danger.

For this reason, an emergency landing on water can only be recommended with landing gear extended, but even then only as a last resort.

Apparently, if the gear is retracted, the glider may touch down, perhaps bounce once, and then take a nose dive for the bottom of the lake! If the water is shallow, the glider may impact on the bottom of the lake. Of course, the glider is very buoyant, and will pop back up to the surface where it will float for a period assuming it is still in one piece.

The dive brakes should be left closed for the slowest touch down speed, and then opened fully at the moment of touchdown to help keep the glider from impacting with the bottom of the lake.

If the tail touches the water first, it will be sucked down into the water. (Touch a spoon to a stream of water coming from a faucet, and you will observe the same effect.) This increases the angle of attack of the wing, causing the glider to climb, rather steeply, and then stall. The nose goes down and the glider strikes the water very much nose down. There is a dramatic film showing this exact sequence. When making a water landing, have the landing gear down, do not touch the tail first, and open the dive brakes at touchdown.

ROUGH COUNTRY

Doris and I were driving across a high desert, southwest of Casper, Wyoming. Two giant thunderstorms with dark columns of water and numerous lightning bolts were split by the highway. High mountains surrounded the valley.

The gentle rolling desert floor was covered by sagebrush, which is a relatively small plant. There were large areas of rocks the size of baseballs. Some areas were devoid of plant life, but were obviously too small to land in.
"What if you had to land in that stuff?" Doris mused.

It was a good question. The plants were not high enough to grab your wing if you were careful and kept the wings level at touchdown. The wind had blown the earth from around each plant, leaving each plant on top of a small mound. As the glider rolled across each plant, the glider would be severely jolted.

The rocks were a major concern. They might not hurt the pilot, but would probably cause damage to the glider.

How to handle the problem?

Every foot the pilot can reduce the ground roll reduces the chance for damage. The glider's slowest possible speed is with the dive brakes closed. An attempt should be made to allow the glider to land with the dive brakes closed, then opening them and applying the wheel brake at the moment of touchdown.

The shortest possible roll out will be an uphill landing. The terrain was gently rolling. Landing uphill was probably the most important consideration to this problem.

There are often dirt roads as well as highways running through this desert terrain, however, these have hazards not easily seen from the air. One of the more serious is the practice of bulldozing the road so it is below the grade of the surrounding desert. This increases the chance of the gliders wings catching on brush or the embankment.

TWO GLIDERS LANDING AT THE SAME MOMENT

You are entering the landing pattern, and discover another glider at the same altitude, also entering the landing pattern. What should you do?

Assume the landing area is narrow so both gliders can not land side by side.

One of the glider pilots needs to take command of the situation by indicating the intention to land first. Increasing airspeed, and/or opening the dive brakes should clearly indicate the other glider pilot should delay as much as possible.

The first glider should then land short, or long, or land and taxi clear of the runway, or land to one side to give plenty of clearance for the other glider. The worst thing that could happen is for the first glider to land and stop in the middle of the runway, blocking the landing area. For this reason, I will try to be the first glider, because I know what to do, and the other pilot might not.

Don't forget the radio if you can communicate with the other glider pilot, or to announce the problem to the people on the ground who may be able to help move the first glider off the landing area.

FENCES AND WIRES

Wire fences and electrical utility wires are a serious problem for glider pilots. They are often very difficult to see. Pilots have been seriously injured and even killed when running into wires. The wire can act just like a cheese slicer, and will cut its way through the skin of the glider or the canopy.

172

I once saw a Schweizer 1-26 that ran into an electric wire. The wire slid up over the nose of the glider, and under the wings. The wire drew tight as it reached the aft portion of the canopy, and sliced its way down through the canopy. The cut was as clean as if it were carefully cut with a fine saw blade. In this case, the pilot was not hurt.

Should you be faced with a wire fence you are going to roll through, it is better to aim for the fence post rather than aiming for a place between the fence posts. The idea is that if you hit the wire hard enough, you may be killed by the wire. If you hit the fence post, the post will probably bend or break, and the glider will roll over the fence.

Telephone and utility wires are sometimes impossible to see from the air. Look for the poles, or the shadow of the poles. Watch for paths cut through a forest for the utility wires. Also, assume there are wires around all fields, and along any road.

GEAR UP LANDING

It is sometimes suggested it might be better to land with the landing gear in the retracted position in some circumstances. Soft dirt, snow, water, wet grass all lend themselves to the suggestion. The problem is the pilot's tailbone is just an inch or so from the outside world. A couple layers of fiberglass, or perhaps a few thousandths of aluminum is all that protects the pilot. Should the glider strike a stone, the pilot's tailbone may be broken, and the pilot may never walk again.

The glider has no value compared to the pilots well being. The landing gear is often the only impact absorbing structure that will prevent injury to the pilot.

There is no time when the glider should be intentionally landed with the landing gear retracted.

LANDING IN TALL CROPS

Should you need to land in a tall crop such as mature corn, land at the minimum possible airspeed to reduce damage to the glider. This means a landing into the wind with the dive brakes closed at the moment of contact.

THE UNAVOIDABLE CRASH

If you know you are going to crash, try to keep the glider flying in a controlled manner. Crash as slow as possible, and with the yaw string straight. Make yourself as small as possible. Pull your legs and feet back. Protect your face and head.

SHORT FIELD

If you have chosen a short landing field, remember the diagonal is longer than a side. It may be better to land diagonally, even though it means landing diagonally across cultivated rows.

DOUBLE RELEASE FAILURE

It is very unlikely an aerotow double release failure will ever happen to you. An unofficial worldwide tally of this event, can account for only three occasions.

Failure of the glider release occurs very rarely, however, frequently enough that all pilots must be trained to know what to do should it happen to them. Lack of required maintenance of the release mechanism, and/or the actuating cable and knob will usually be the prime cause of a release failure. This can often be detected during a thorough preflight inspection. Tow release mechanisms must be overhauled periodically. Another possibility is the use of an improper tow ring on the end of the tow rope. (Do not use chain links!)

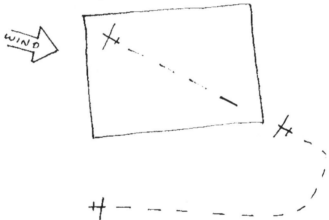

A possible scenario might have the release knob come off in the pilot's hand when the pilot reaches release altitude. Knowledge about the glider might offer the pilot another alternative method of actuating the release mechanism without the knob.

Release failure on the tow plane is also very unlikely, and will generally fall under the same circumstances as the glider. On two of the three known double release failures, the cause of the tow plane failure was an inadvertent knot formed by the tow rope as the tow plane turned in front of the parked glider preceding the launch. The tailwheel picked up the rope, and the rope tied a half-hitch around the tail wheel assembly, making the release ineffective. (Tow planes should never taxi over the tow rope.)

OK, you can't release. What should you do? If the glider and tow plane have a radio, it should be used to discuss the problem. If no operating radio is available, the standard signal that the glider pilot uses to indicate a release failure is to move to the side and rock the glider's wings. Which side?

The rule is to move to either side. Suppose the tow pilot has made many tows during this day. It is the kind of day when nearly everyone is releasing at 2,000 feet AGL. There are several other gliders waiting to be launched. The tow plane nears 2,000 feet. The tow pilot is expecting the glider to release and *turn right*.

(You're already ahead of me, aren't you?)

The glider pilot pulls on the release knob, and the knob comes off in his or her hand. "Oh my God an emergency!' The glider pilot begins to move to the right to give the signal. The tow pilot sees the glider moving to the right, and, thinking the glider has released, begins a rapid descent, pulling the wings off of the glider. (There is a possibility this scenario has actually happened on more than one occasion.)

The glider should move to the *left* to give the signal.

Have you ever practiced performing this signal? It is not easy! Every pilot should be given the opportunity to perform this signal (as well as all other signals) while accompanied by a qualified instructor. If you are an instructor, consider making all pilots who need flight checks and BFR's perform these signals. Be sure to coordinate this with the tow pilot.

Moving to the left and *gently* rocking the wings of the glider will get the attention of the tow pilot sooner or later. The tow pilot will probably first think it is a signal to turn right, but at least will not likely to begin a descent. If the tow pilot makes a right turn, the glider pilot gives the signal again, etc. until the tow pilot actually looks back in the mirror, or turns around to see what the dickens is going on back there. In many cases, the tow pilot sees a signal never seen before.

The tow pilot will finally understand the glider pilot must be having some kind of difficulty and just may not be able to release. As a glider pilot, you must understand the type of training many tow pilots have had. Also, the lack of recurrent training means many, if not most, tow pilots don't know all (any) of the standard signals. If you have this emergency, you can expect some confusion on the tow pilot's part. You should be patient. Give repeated signals if necessary. Do not resort to violent, or extreme signal displays.

If the tow release or ring is jammed for some reason, maneuvering the glider by yawing to one side or the other, or shaking the nose with small, rapid stick and/or rudder movements while holding the release knob in the fully deployed position, may free up the mechanism. Intentionally putting a small amount of slack in the rope, and pulling on the release knob may also help. Try the release mechanism frequently while the emergency continues in case it should decide to work.

If either aircraft has a working radio, the folks on the ground should be notified of the emergency. The tow plane is supposed to return to the area of the gliderport and release the tow rope. The rope will fall down and back beneath the glider, and in some cases the resulting back pressure will release itself. The tow pilot should take this into consideration so the rope doesn't fall on people or property, causing injury or damage.

The glider pilot would probably then land with the tow rope still attached. (Don't forget to continue to try the release.) Observers on the ground might be able to see the tow rope still attached to the glider, and radio this information to the glider pilot. The glider pilot must assume the rope is attached and land with extra altitude to be sure to clear all obstructions in the landing pattern.

If the glider is carrying water ballast, it should be dumped during this emergency.

In case of a double release failure, the tow pilot would make the discovery that the tow plane's release had failed after radioing the ground and attempting to release the glider. In other words, there would be a delay after the glider pilot gave the first signal.

The standard procedure after the tow plane has given the "I can't release either" signal (wagging the tow plane's rudder), is for the glider to move to the low tow position. The reason for this is a safety matter, not an aerodynamic, or landing matter. The tow plane has the capability of descending much quicker than the glider. Should the tow plane descend too fast, the glider will end up in a position very much too high above the tow plane , which lifts the tail of the tow plane making the problem worse. This is likely to result in the tow plane diving towards the earth in an uncontrollable fashion. It may not be possible to recover from this position. Even momentary lapses in the tow plane pilot's skills and procedures could lead to disaster. A simple distraction (very likely considering the circumstances) could cause the tow pilot to allow the tow plane to begin to descend too quickly, making it impossible for the glider to match the descent rate.

Because of this potential hazard, the glider pilot moves to the low tow position, after receiving the "I can't release either" signal from the tow plane. The low tow position gives the glider pilot more time to react should the tow pilot begin to descend faster than desirable. The glider pilot will have more time to deploy dive brakes, side slip, or both. Use of the glider's dive brakes during the descent is almost always required to prevent slack from forming in the tow rope.

The tow plane should descend slowly. How slow? As slow as possible. What's the hurry? The only reason to get down quickly is if the tow plane is running out of gas. In any case, the tow pilot must understand it is not possible for the glider to descend as quickly as the tow plane, and the tow pilot's life depends on the glider being able to descend at the same rate. If it was my butt in the seat of the tow plane, I'd descend very slowly.

The tow plane should radio the ground about the emergency, and make a very wide landing pattern with very gentle turns. A very long final approach is desirable. The turn onto final approach would probably be a mile or more from the end of the runway.

The tow plane and glider approach the end of the runway. As they get closer to the earth, the glider is forced to allow the tow plane to descend (relative to the glider's position) until the glider is level and at the same height above the ground as the tow plane. The typical tow plane will normally land at a slightly faster airspeed than the glider, however this speed differential is seldom great, and the glider pilot should land at the same time using most, if not full, dive brakes. Forcing the glider on the ground prematurely could cause P.I.O.'s which might cause loss of control.

The tow plane and glider should plan to roll to a stop with little, or no usage of the wheel brake. The most likely problem is a collision as the two aircraft roll to a stop. Most glider wheel brakes are just barely adequate to stop the glider by itself. It is unreasonable for the glider pilot to attempt to stop both the glider and tow plane with the glider's wheel brake. Save the brake and only use it if absolutely necessary.

In case of a collision on the ground, the glider will probably run into the tow plane causing some damage to both aircraft. Frankly, aircraft are expendable. They have no value compared to the lives they contain. There is a real possibility of the tow plane pilot losing control and ground looping the tow plane during the landing, or roll-out phase. If this should happen, the propeller becomes a giant meat slicer. Should the glider run into this, the pilot could be seriously injured or killed.

As the tow plane is touching down, it might be wise for the tow pilot to turn the magnetos off to stop the engine and allow the tow plane to roll to a stop.

During discussions about this potential emergency, someone always comes up with the idea to break the rope instead of using the above procedure. This idea is not suggested by any text in any country of the world. The problem is, if you fail to break the rope, you can end up with a situation that is far more dangerous, perhaps life threatening to both aircraft. Landing together, turns out to be rather easy and safe if the pilots of both aircraft have at least minimal training.

All pilots should be given the opportunity to make a descent of perhaps 500 feet or so during training, so they can experience this simple procedure. Low tow should be a part of normal flight training. Since the probability of a double release failure is so low, and there are real risks, although slight, to landing while on tow, it is probably better to only practice the low tow descent at altitude, rather than a complete low tow descent, pattern and landing.

CHAPTER 32

GLIDER AEROBATICS

WARNING: Never attempt to teach yourself aerobatics. Get an experienced instructor.

Most gliders are built with no consideration of the structural limitations, or the special loads placed on an aircraft during aerobatic flight. As a pilot you should know the glider you fly may have never been tested by qualified individuals for the type of aerobatic maneuver you may be contemplating.

With their long wings, and corresponding slow roll rates, rolling motions are particularly difficult. Attempting rolling motions can cause structural failure of the ailerons, wings, or control linkages. It is also possible to damage the fuselage and tail if the glider falls sideways out of an improper roll or other aerobatic maneuver. If you want to do serious aerobatics, it is far better to use a powered aircraft that is built for that kind of activity.

Most gliders are permitted to perform simple aerobatic maneuvers. There is often a cockpit placard indicating what maneuvers are permitted and the recommended entry speeds. If there is no placard, check the flight manual for any restrictions. Chandelles and lazy eights are particularly beautiful maneuvers when done properly, and demand a great deal of pilot skill to accomplish them correctly.

At no time during these maneuvers should the glider be climbing so steeply that a tail slide is possible. A tail slide will almost certainly damage the control surfaces and can disable the glider entirely. Limit your pitch up attitude to no more than 60 degrees. If, during aerobatics, a very steep stall or tail slide is imminent, you should centralize the controls and hold them with both hands and feet very firmly to try to keep the control surfaces from flapping hard against their hinges.

Inverted flight can be hazardous. If a glider is upside down, as in the top of a loop, and the speed is excessive, then the glider can not be stopped from accelerating past the never exceed, or even the maximum design speed, as it finishes the second half of the loop.

CHANDELLE

A "chandelle" is a climbing turn beginning from approximately straight-and-level flight, and ending at the completion of 180 degrees of turn in a wings-level, nose-high attitude at the minimum controllable airspeed. The maneuver demands the maximum flight performance of the glider be obtained; that is, the glider should gain the most altitude possible for a given degree of bank and entry speed without stalling. However, since numerous atmospheric variables beyond the control of the pilot will effect the specific amount of altitude gained, the altitude gain is not a criterion of the quality of the maneuver.

Prior to starting a chandelle, the airspace behind and above should be checked clear of other traffic. A reference point 90 degrees from the flight path should be chosen. A chandelle should be started at any speed recommended by the manufacturer — in most cases not above the glider's design maneuvering speed.

After the appropriate airspeed has been established in a shallow, wings level dive, the chandelle is started by smoothly entering a coordinated turn with an angle of bank appropriate for the glider being flown. Normally, this angle of bank should not exceed 30 degrees. After the appropriate bank is established, it should remain constant until 90 degrees of turn is completed. Meanwhile, a climbing turn should be started by smoothly applying back elevator pressure to increase the pitch attitude at a constant rate and to attain the highest pitch attitude as 90 degrees of turn is completed. Although the degree of bank is fixed during this climbing turn, it may appear to increase, and in fact, actually will tend to increase if allowed to do so as the maneuver continues.

When the turn has progressed 90 degrees from the original heading, the pilot should begin rolling out of the bank at a constant rate while maintaining a constant pitch attitude. Since the angle of bank will be decreasing during the roll out, the vertical component of lift will increase slightly. For this reason, it may be necessary to release a slight amount of back elevator pressure in order to keep the nose of the glider from rising too high.

As the wings are being leveled at the completion of 180 degrees of turn, the pitch attitude should be noted by checking the outside references. This pitch attitude should be held momentarily while the glider is at the minimum controllable airspeed. Then the pitch attitude may be gently reduced to return to straight-and-level gliding flight.

To roll out of a left chandelle, the left aileron must be lowered to raise the left wing. This creates more drag than the aileron on the right wing, resulting in a tendency for the glider to yaw to the left. To maintain coordinated flight, considerable right rudder pressure must be used during the roll out to overcome the effects of aileron drag.

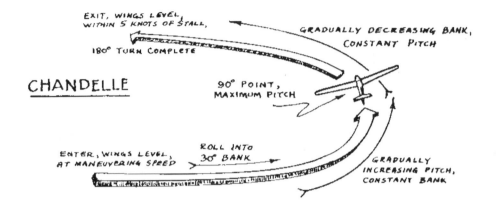

EXIT, WINGS LEVEL,
WITHIN 5 KNOTS OF STALL,

GRADUALLY DECREASING BANK,
CONSTANT PITCH

180° TURN COMPLETE

CHANDELLE

90° POINT,
MAXIMUM PITCH

ENTER, WINGS LEVEL,
AT MANEUVERING SPEED

ROLL INTO
30° BANK

GRADUALLY
INCREASING PITCH,
CONSTANT BANK

LAZY EIGHT

This maneuver derives its name from the manner in which the extended longitudinal axis of the glider is made to trace a flight pattern in the form of a figure 8 lying on its side (a "lazy" 8). The objective of the Lazy 8 is to develop the pilot's feel for varying control forces, and the ability to plan and remain oriented while maneuvering the glider with positive, accurate control. It requires constantly changing control pressures necessitated by changing combinations of climbing and descending turns at varying airspeeds. This maneuver can be used to develop and demonstrate the pilot's mastery of the glider in maximum performance flight situations.

A lazy 8 consists of two 180 degree turns, in opposite directions, while making a climb and a descent in a symmetrical pattern during each of the turns. At no time throughout the Lazy 8 is the glider flown straight and level — instead, it is rolled directly from one bank to the other with the wings level only at the moment the turn is reversed at the completion of each 180 degree change in heading.

As an aid to making symmetrical loops of the 8 during each turn, prominent reference points should be selected on the horizon. The reference points selected should be 45 degrees, 90 degrees, and 135 degrees from the direction in which the maneuver is begun.

180

Prior to performing a Lazy 8, the airspace behind and above should be clear of other air traffic. The maneuver should be entered from a slight dive to the airspeed recommended by the manufacturer, or at the glider's design maneuvering speed.

The maneuver is started with a gradual climbing turn in the direction of the 45 degree reference point. The climbing turn should be planned and controlled so that the maximum pitch-up attitude is reached at the 45 degree point. The rate of rolling into the bank must be such as to prevent the rate of turn from becoming too rapid. As the pitch attitude is raised, the airspeed decreases, causing the rate of turn to increase. Since the bank also is being increased, it too causes the rate of turn to increase. Unless the maneuver is begun with a slow rate of roll, the combination of increasing pitch and increasing bank will cause the rate of turn to be so rapid that the 45 degree reference point will be reached before the highest pitch attitude is attained.

At the 45 degree point, the pitch attitude should be at maximum and the angle of bank continuing to increase. Also at the 45 degree point, the pitch attitude should start to decrease slowly toward the horizon and the 90 degree reference point.

As the glider's nose is being lowered toward the 90 degree reference point, the bank should continue to increase. Due to the decreasing airspeed, a slight amount of opposite aileron pressure may be required to prevent the bank from becoming too steep. When the aircraft completes 90 degrees of the turn, the bank should be at the maximum angle (approximately 30 degrees), the airspeed should be at its minimum (5 to 10 knots above stall speed), and the glider pitch attitude should be passing through level flight. At this time an imaginary line, extending from the pilot's eye and parallel to the longitudinal axis of the glider, passes through the 90 degree reference point.

Lazy 8's normally should be performed with no more than approximately a 30 degree bank. Steeper banks may be used, but control touch and technique must be developed to a much higher degree than when the maneuver is performed with a shallower bank.

The pilot should not hesitate at this point but should continue to fly the glider into a descending turn so that the glider's nose describes the same size loop below the horizon as it did above. As the pilot's reference line passes through the 90 degree point, the bank should be decreased gradually, and the glider's nose allowed to continue lowering. When the glider has turned 135 degrees, the nose should be in its lowest pitch attitude. The airspeed will be increasing during this descending turn so it will be necessary to gradually relax rudder and aileron pressure and to simultaneously raise the nose and roll the wings level. As this is being accomplished, the pilot should note the amount of turn remaining and adjust the rate of roll out and pitch change so that the wings become level and the original airspeed is attained in level flight just as the 180 degree point is reached. Upon reaching that point, a climbing turn should be started immediately in the opposite direction toward the selected references points to complete the second half of the eight in the same manner as the first half.

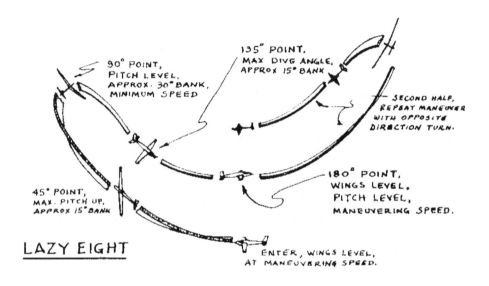

90° POINT,
PITCH LEVEL,
APPROX. 30° BANK,
MINIMUM SPEED

135° POINT,
MAX DIVE ANGLE,
APPROX 15° BANK

SECOND HALF,
REPEAT MANEUVER
WITH OPPOSITE
DIRECTION TURN.

45° POINT,
MAX. PITCH UP,
APPROX 15° BANK

180° POINT,
WINGS LEVEL,
PITCH LEVEL,
MANEUVERING SPEED.

LAZY EIGHT

ENTER, WINGS LEVEL,
AT MANEUVERING SPEED.

182

Pierce Brosnan, "The Thomas Crown Affair"
in Schempp-Hirth Duo Discus.

CHAPTER 33

ABC BADGES

In an effort to standardize flight training programs, a series of badges has been established. These badges are administered by the Soaring Society Of America, and are awarded by SSA instructors.

Requirements for the A Badge include:

Preflight phase:

1. Sailplane nomenclature.
2. Sailplane handling procedures.
3. Sailplane preflight check.
4. Airport rules and FAR's.
5. Tow equipment signals and procedures.
6. Hookup of tow rope or cable.
7. Take off signals.
8. Pilot responsibilities.

Applicant holds:

1. Valid FAA student pilots certificate.
2. Suitable logbook.

Pre-solo phase:

Applicant has completed the following minimum flight training program:

1. Familiarization flight.
2. Cockpit check procedure.
3. Effects of controls, on the ground and in flight.
4. Takeoff procedure, crosswind takeoffs.
5. Flight during tow.
6. Straight and level flight.
7. Simple turns.
8. Circuit procedure and landing patterns.
9. Landing procedure, downwind, crosswind landings.
10. Moderate and steep turns up to 720 degrees.
11. Stalls and stall recoveries.
12. Conditions of spin entry and spin recovery.
13. Effective use of spoilers/flaps and slips.
14. Emergency procedures.
15. Oral exam on FAR's.
16. Solo Flight.

THE B BADGE:

Demonstration of soaring ability by solo flight at least 30 minutes duration after release from a 2,000 foot tow. Add 1 1/2 minutes for each additional 100 ft. above 2,000 ft.

THE C BADGE

Recognizes the pilot's potential ability for cross country flight. The requirements for the C Badge are:

Pre-cross country phase.

1. Dual soaring practice, including instruction in techniques for soaring thermals, ridges and waves. (Simulated flight and/or ground instruction may be used when suitable conditions do not exist.)

2. Have knowledge of:
   a. Cross country procedures.
   b. Glider assembly, disassembly and retrieving.
   c. Dangers of cross country flying.

3. Solo practice. (Two hours minimum.)

4. Demonstrate soaring ability by a solo flight of at least 60 minutes duration after release from a 2,000 ft. (or lower) tow. (Add 1 1/2 minutes for each additional 100 ft. above 2,000 ft. tow.)

5. While accompanied by an SSA instructor, demonstrate ability to:
   a. Make a simulated off field landing approach, without reference to an altimeter.
   b. Perform an accuracy landing from the approach, touching down and coming to a complete stop within an area 500 ft. in length.

Note: The approach to the airport will begin at least 1 mile from the field and at an altitude sufficiently high to safely complete the maneuver and landing. The boundaries of the landing area will be specified by the instructor.

THE BRONZE BADGE

1. Complete the ABC program with the C Badge awarded.

2. Log at least 15 solo hours in gliders, including 30 solo flights of which at least 10 are flown in a single place glider.

3. Log at least two flights each which have two hours duration or more.

4. Perform at least three solo spot landings in a glider witnessed by an SSA instructor. The accuracy and distance parameters are based on the glider's performance, current winds, runway surface condition, and density altitude. As a guideline, a minimum distance of 400 feet would be acceptable for a Schweizer 2-33. (This is a land and stop in a specified zone requirement.)

5. Log dual time in gliders with an instructor during which at least two accuracy landings (same as above) were made without reference to an altimeter to simulate off-field and strange field landings.

6. Pass a closed book written examination covering cross-country techniques and knowledge. Minimum passing grade is 80%.

It is important to complete the entire ABC badges, the Bronze Badge, the Silver Altitude requirement (1000 meter altitude gain) and the five hour Duration require-ment before you consider flying cross country. Completing all of these requirements demonstrates you have developed the minimum flying skills and knowledge neces-sary to fly cross country. These awards have been developed to help you develop your flying skills before you attempt any actual cross country flying.

The three accuracy landings as stated in item four are three successful landings in a row, from three different patterns, left hand, right hand, and downwind. The down-wind landing would be done with little or no wind. The intention of the two landings with an instructor in item five, is they should be done at a strange site, such as another airport that the student is not familiar.

CHAPTER 34

FAI SOARING AWARDS

The Silver Badge, Gold Badge, and Gold badge with Diamonds are soaring awards granted to pilots for flights that satisfy the qualifications of each badge as set forth in the sporting code of The Federation Aeronautique Internationale (FAI).

QUALIFICATIONS AND REQUIREMENTS

SILVER BADGE

Distance: a straight flight of at least 50 km (31.1 miles).

Duration: a flight of at least 5 hours.

Height: a gain in height of at least 1000 meters (3281 feet).

The distance leg may be an out to a pre-declared point and return to the starting point by following the rules specified in the FAI code. The total distance covered is a minimum of 100 kilometers for this out and return flight. Also, if a triangle is declared with one leg more than 50 km, it can qualify for the Silver Distance requirement. A preflight declaration must be made and photographs taken. See the SSA handbook for further details.

GOLD BADGE

Distance: a flight of at leas t 300 kilometers (186.4 miles).

Duration: a flight of at least 5 hours.

Height: a gain in height of at least 3,000 meters (9842 feet).

DIAMOND BADGE

There are 3 diamonds:

Diamond Goal: a flight of at least 300 kilometers (186.4 miles) over a triangular or an out and return course.

Diamond Distance: a flight of at least 500 kilometers (310.7 miles)

Diamond Height: a gain in height of at least 5,000 meters (16,404 feet).

1,000 KILOMETER BADGE

The FAI awards a special badge and diploma to pilots achieving a distance flight of at least 1,000 kilometers (621 miles).

THE SOARING SOCIETY OF AMERICA

The SSA is a nonprofit organization of enthusiasts who seek to foster and promote all phases of soaring flight. It supervises FAI related activities such as record attempts, competition sanctions, and the FAI badge program.

The journal of the Soaring Society is *Soaring Magazine*.

You will want to join this organization by sending for membership forms at the following address:

SSA
PO Box E
Hobbs, New Mexico, 88241

CHAPTER 35

CONTEST AND RECORD FLYING

Most glider pilots rarely leave the immediate area surrounding the gliderport. For many this is enough. To soar among the clouds is a supreme form of relaxation and enjoyment.

For others, badge flying opens a whole new aspect of the sport. For a small percentage, record flying and competition flying, is the goal.

As you proceed through the flight training program, and the ABC & Bronze badges, you will probably develop at least a passing interest in earning your Silver, Gold and Diamond badges. While earning these, you will probably look at the record book and discover that many state soaring records are easily within your capabilities.

As you climb in a thermal at the local gliderport, it is almost impossible to not find yourself competing against another glider pilot to see who is going to out climb the other. Eventually you will feel good about your developing skills and might purchase a share of a glider so you can fly with fewer restrictions than flying a rental or club glider. You might join a few friends in a "friendly" task flying around nearby turnpoints near the gliderport.

Competition begins with these friendly match-ups and weekend task settings. The next step might be a formally organized "Little Guys Meet" for beginning contest pilots. The next level is a Regional contest.

National soaring contests establish the champions of each class of sailplanes, Open, 15 meter, Standard, Sports, World and 1-26 classes. The Open class permits any size sailplane. The 15 Meter Class sailplanes (sometimes called the "Racing Class") are only limited to wing span. The Standard Class is also limited to 15 meters and may not have flaps or other airfoil changing devises. There are also club class contests where a handicap factor permits sailplanes of various performance capabilities to compete with one another, and one-design competition such as the World or 1-26 contests.

Competition in today's contests is a race against time. At the beginning of each day, the competition committee evaluates the day and sets a task that most pilots are able to complete. These tasks are usually triangular courses, or out and return tasks. Quadrilaterals (many-sided shapes) are becoming increasing popular because they keep the pilots relatively close to the gliderport. Task lengths will vary from approximately 60 miles to as much as 400 miles. Each days winner has completed the task in the shortest time and all others are given scores reflecting their slower speeds. A contest will run for 5 to 14 days, but because of inclement weather, a contest won't count unless a minimum of 2 or 3 days are flown.

Competition pilots are very skillful. It is quite humbling to fly against the top pilots in a formal contest and have them beat you around a course by many minutes, at a speed several miles an hour faster than you. To develop those skills necessary to place in the top 10 of a national contest requires dedication, and hours of practice.

Most pilots never make it to this level. It is a phenomenal challenge, but it is a lot of fun too. Soaring contests are filled with good fellowship, bar-b-cues, and social get-togethers.

Record flying is different. You select the day you will attempt a record flight. It will be a superb soaring day and you will try to make the most of it. It is often a day, or a task where you are the only person flying. It is you against the elements.

The world records are the ultimate achievements by the top soaring pilots of the world. National records are usually out of the reach of beginning cross country soaring pilots. But the state, regional, or even gliderport or club records are well within the grasp of low time pilots. If you are able to earn just one of the certificates awarded for a state record, you will be on your way to set more records.

CHAPTER 36

THE FLIGHT TEST

Much of your flight training has been in preparation for the private pilot flight test. (See Flight Training Syllabus in the front of this book.) The flight test consists of the oral test and the practical, or flight test.

Most of the following information was adapted from the government document, *Private Pilot Practical Test Standards* (FAA-S-8081-22, dated April, 1999.) It is available through the internet at: www.fedworld.gov/pub/faa-att/html. A copy is provide in the following pages.+

During the test you will be asked questions about your general knowledge of Federal Aviation Regulations, navigation, weather, operational procedures, signals, safety precautions, preflight, ground and/or aerotow, turns, glider performance speeds, stalls, accuracy landings and approaches.

The flight test will consist of your ability to perform the required pilot operations based on the following:

1. Executing TASKS within the aircraft's performance capabilities and limitations, including the aircraft's systems;

2. Executing emergency procedures and maneuvers appropriate to the aircraft;

3. Piloting the aircraft with smoothness and accuracy.

4. Exercising good judgment.

5. Applying aeronautical knowledge. and

6. Showing mastery of the aircraft, within the standards outline, with the successful outcome of a TASK never seriously in doubt.

If you should fail any one of the TASKS, you fail the flight test.

The complete Private Glider Practical Test Standards are included in the following pages.

U.S. Department of Transportation
Federal Aviation Administration

PRIVATE PILOT
Practical Test Standards
for Glider

FAA-S-8081-22
APRIL, 1999

FLIGHT STANDARDS SERVICE
Washington, DC 20591

NOTE

Material in FAA-S-8081-22 is effective April 1, 1999. All previous editions of the Private Pilot—Glider Practical Test Standards are obsolete as of this date.

FOREWORD

The Private Pilot—Glider Practical Test Standards (PTS) book has been published by the Federal Aviation Administration (FAA) to establish the standards for private pilot certification practical tests for the glider category. FAA inspectors and designated pilot examiners shall conduct practical tests in compliance with these standards. Flight instructors and applicants should find these standards helpful during training and when preparing for practical tests.

L. Nicholas Lacey
Director, Flight Standards Service

CONTENTS

194

INTRODUCTION

General Information

The Flight Standards Service of the Federal Aviation Administration (FAA) has developed this practical test book as a standard to be used by FAA inspectors and designated pilot examiners when conducting private pilot—glider practical tests. Flight instructors are expected to use this book when preparing applicants for practical tests. Applicants should be familiar with this book and refer to these standards during their training.

Information considered directive in nature is described in this practical test book in terms, such as "shall" and "must" indicating the actions are mandatory. Guidance information is described in terms, such as "should" and "may" indicating the actions are desirable or permissive, but not mandatory.

The FAA gratefully acknowledges the valuable assistance provided by many individuals and organizations throughout the aviation community who contributed their time and talent in assisting with the revision of these practical test standards.

These practical test standards may be accessed through the Internet at www.fedworld.gov/pub/faa-att/faa-att.htm, or by modem at 703-321-3339. You may purchase these standards from the Superintendent of Documents, U.S. Government Printing Office, Washington, DC 20402.

Changes to these standards, in accordance with AC 60-27, Announcement of Availability: Changes to Practical Test Standards, will be available through the Internet and then later incorporated into a printed revision. For a listing of changes, AFS-600's Internet web site may be accessed at www.mmac.jccbi.gov/afs/afs600.htm.

Comments regarding this publication should be sent to:

U.S. Department of Transportation
Federal Aviation Administration
Flight Standards Service
Airman Testing Standards Branch, AFS-630
P.O. Box 25082
Oklahoma City, OK 73125

Practical Test Standard Concept

Title 14 of the Code of Federal Regulations (14 CFR) part 61 specifies the areas in which knowledge and skill must be demonstrated by the applicant before the issuance of a private pilot certificate or rating. The CFR's provide the flexibility to permit the FAA to publish practical test standards containing the AREAS OF OPERATION and specific TASKS in which pilot competency shall be demonstrated. The FAA shall revise this book whenever it is determined that changes are needed in the interest of safety. Adherence to the provisions of the regulations and the practical test standards is mandatory for the evaluation of private pilot applicants.

Test Book Description

This test book contains the practical test standards for private pilot—glider. This includes the AREAS OF OPERATION and TASKS required for the issuance of an initial private pilot—glider certificate and for the addition of category ratings.

Practical Test Standards Description

AREAS OF OPERATION are phases of the practical test arranged in a logical sequence within each standard. They begin with Preflight Preparation and end with Postflight Procedures. The examiner, however, may conduct the practical test in any sequence that results in a complete and efficient test.

TASKS are titles of knowledge areas, flight procedures, or maneuvers appropriate to an AREA OF OPERATION.

NOTE is used to emphasize special considerations required in the AREA OF OPERATION or TASK.

REFERENCE identifies the publication(s) that describe(s) the TASK. Descriptions of TASKS are not included in the standards because this information can be found in the current issue of the listed reference. Publications other than those listed may be used for references if their content conveys substantially the same meaning as the referenced publications.

These practical test standards are based on the following references.

14 CFR part 43 Maintenance, Preventive Maintenance, Rebuilding, and Alteration
14 CFR part 61 Certification: Pilots, Flight Instructors, and Ground Instructors
14 CFR part 91 General Operating and Flight Rules
AC 00-6 Aviation Weather
AC 00-45 Aviation Weather Services
AC 61-21 Flight Training Handbook
AC 61-23 Pilot's Handbook of Aeronautical Knowledge
AC 61-65 Certification: Pilots and Flight Instructors
AC 61-84 Role of Preflight Preparation
AC 90-48 Pilots' Role in Collision Avoidance

AC 90-66 Recommended Standard Traffic Patterns and Practices for Aeronautical Operations At Airports Without Operating Control Towers.

AIM Aeronautical Information Manual

AFD Airport Facility Directory

NOTAM's Notices to Airmen

Other Soaring Flight Manual (Jeppeson Sanderson) Glider Flight Manual

The Objective lists the important elements that must be satisfactorily performed to demonstrate competency in a TASK. The Objective includes:

> 1. specifically what the applicant should be able to do;
> 2. conditions under which the TASK is to be performed; and
> 3. acceptable performance standards.

Use of the Practical Test Standards Book

The FAA requires that all practical tests be conducted in accordance with the appropriate practical test standards and the policies set forth in the INTRODUCTION. Applicants shall be evaluated in ALL TASKS included in each AREA OF OPERATION of the appropriate practical test standard, unless otherwise noted.

An applicant who holds a private pilot certificate seeking an additional glider category rating, will be evaluated in at least the AREAS OF OPERATION and TASKS listed in the Additional Rating Task Table located on page 9 of this practical test standard. At the discretion of the examiner, an evaluation of the applicant's competence in the remaining AREAS OF OPERATION and TASKS may be conducted.

In preparation for each practical test, the examiner shall develop a written "plan of action." The "plan of action" shall include all TASKS in each AREA OF OPERATION, unless noted otherwise. If the elements in one TASK have already been evaluated in another TASK, they need not be repeated. For example, the "plan of action" need not include evaluating the applicant on complying with markings, signals, and clearances at the end of the flight, if that element was sufficiently observed at the beginning of the flight. Any TASKS selected for evaluation during a practical test shall be evaluated in its entirety.

The examiner is not required to follow the precise order in which the AREAS OF OPERATION and TASKS appear in this book. The examiner may change the sequence or combine TASKS with similar Objectives to have an orderly and efficient flow of the practical test. For example, Boxing The Wake may be combined with Maintaining Tow Positions. The examiner's "plan of action" shall include the order and combination of TASKS to be demonstrated by the applicant in a manner that will result in an efficient and valid test.

Examiners shall place special emphasis upon those aircraft operations that are most critical to flight safety. Among these areas are precise aircraft control and sound judgment in decision making. Although these areas may or may not be shown under each TASK, they are essential to flight safety and shall receive careful evaluation throughout the practical test. If these areas are shown in the Objective, additional emphasis shall be placed on them. The examiner shall also emphasize stall/spin awareness, wake turbulence avoidance, low-level wind shear, collision avoidance, runway incursion avoidance, and checklist usage.

The examiner is expected to use good judgment in the performance of simulated emergency procedures. The use of the safest means for simulation is expected. Consideration must be given to local conditions, both meteorological and topographical, at the time of the test, as well as the applicant's workload, and the condition of the aircraft used. If the procedure being evaluated would put the maneuver in jeopardy, it is expected that the applicant will simulate that portion of the maneuver.

Practical Test Prerequisites

An applicant for the private pilot—glider practical test is required by 14 CFR part 61 to:

1. be at least 16 years of age;
2. be able to read, speak, write, and understand the English language. If there is a doubt, use AC 60-28, English Language Skill Standards;
3. hold at least a student pilot certificate;
4. have passed the appropriate private pilot knowledge test(s) since the beginning of the 24th month before the month in which he or she takes the practical test;
5. have satisfactorily accomplished the required training and obtained the aeronautical experience prescribed;
6. have an endorsement from an authorized instructor certifying that the applicant has received flight training time within 60 days preceding the date of application in preparation for the practical test, and is prepared for the practical test; and
7. also have an endorsement certifying that the applicant has demonstrated satisfactory knowledge of the subject areas in which the applicant was deficient on the airman knowledge test.

Aircraft and Equipment Required for the Practical Test

The private pilot—glider applicant is required by 14 CFR section 61.45, to provide an airworthy, certificated aircraft for use during the practical test. This section further requires that the aircraft must:

1. have fully functioning dual controls, except as provided for in 14 CFR section 61.45(c) and (e); and
2. be capable of performing all AREAS OF OPERATION appropriate to the rating sought and have no operating limitations which prohibit its use in any of the AREAS OF OPERATION required for the practical test.

Flight Instructor Responsibility

An appropriately rated flight instructor is responsible for training the private pilot applicant to acceptable standards in **all** subject matter areas, procedures, and maneuvers included in the TASKS within each AREA OF OPERATION in this practical test standard.

Because of the impact of their teaching activities in developing safe, proficient pilots, flight instructors should exhibit a high level of knowledge, skill, and the ability to impart that knowledge and skill to students.

Throughout the applicant's training, the flight instructor is responsible for emphasizing the performance of effective visual scanning and collision avoidance procedures.

Examiner Responsibility

The examiner conducting the practical test is responsible for determining that the applicant meets the acceptable standards of knowledge and skill of each TASK within the appropriate practical test standard. Since there is no formal division between the "oral" and "skill" portions of the practical test, this becomes an ongoing process throughout the test. Oral questioning, to determine the applicant's knowledge of TASKS and related safety factors, should be used judiciously at all times, especially during the flight portion of the practical test.

During the flight portion of the practical test, the examiner shall evaluate the applicant's use of visual scanning and collision avoidance procedures.

Satisfactory Performance

Satisfactory performance to meet the requirements for certification is based on the applicant's ability to safely:

1. perform the TASKS specified in the AREAS OF OPERATION for the certificate or rating sought within the approved standards;
2. demonstrate mastery of the aircraft with the successful outcome of each TASK performed never seriously in doubt;
3. demonstrate satisfactory proficiency and competency within the approved standards; and
4. demonstrate sound judgment.

Unsatisfactory Performance

If, in the judgment of the examiner, the applicant does not meet the standards of performance of any TASK performed, the associated AREA OF OPERATION is failed and therefore, the practical test is failed. The examiner or applicant may discontinue the test at any time when the failure of an AREA OF OPERATION makes the applicant ineligible for the certificate or rating sought. The test may be continued ONLY with the consent of the applicant. If the test is discontinued, the applicant is entitled to credit for only those AREAS OF OPERATION and TASKS satisfactorily performed; however, during the retest, and at the discretion of the examiner, any TASK may be re-evaluated, including those previously passed.

The word "examiner" is used throughout the standards to denote either the FAA inspector or FAA designated pilot examiner who conducts an official practical test.

Typical areas of unsatisfactory performance and grounds for disqualification are:

1. Any action or lack of action by the applicant that requires corrective intervention by the examiner to maintain safe flight.
2. Failure to use proper and effective visual scanning techniques to clear the area before and while performing maneuvers.
3. Consistently exceeding tolerances stated in the Objectives.
4. Failure to take prompt corrective action when tolerances are exceeded.

When a notice of disapproval is issued, the examiner shall record the applicant's unsatisfactory performance in terms of the AREA OF OPERATION and specific TASK failed or TASK(S) not accomplished.

The AREA(S) OF OPERATION not tested and the number of practical test failures shall also be recorded.

Crew Resource Management (CRM)

CRM refers to the effective use of all available resources: human resources, hardware, and information. Human resources include all groups routinely working with the cockpit crew or pilot who are involved with decisions that are required to operate a flight safely. These groups include, but are not limited to dispatchers, cabin crewmembers, maintenance personnel, air traffic controllers, and weather services. CRM is not a single TASK, but a set of competencies that must be evident in all TASKS in this practical test standard as applied to either crew or single pilot operations.

Applicant's Use of Checklists

Throughout the practical test, the applicant is evaluated on the use of an appropriate checklist. Proper use is dependent on the specific TASK being evaluated. The situation may be such that the use of the checklist, while accomplishing elements of an Objective, would be either unsafe or impractical, especially in a single-pilot operation. In this case, a review of the checklist after the elements have been accomplished, would be appropriate. Division of attention and proper visual scanning should be considered when using a checklist.

Use of Distractions During Practical Tests

Numerous studies indicate that many accidents have occurred when the pilot has been distracted during critical phases of flight. To evaluate the applicant's ability to utilize proper control technique while dividing attention both inside and/or outside the cockpit, the examiner shall cause a realistic distraction during the flight portion of the practical test to evaluate the applicant's ability to divide attention while maintaining safe flight.

Positive Exchange of Flight Controls

During flight training, there must always be a clear understanding between students and flight instructors of who has control of the aircraft. Prior to flight, a briefing should be conducted that includes the procedure for the exchange of flight controls. A positive three-step process in the exchange of flight controls between pilots is a proven procedure and one that is strongly recommended.

When the instructor wishes the student to take control of the aircraft, he or she will say, "You have the flight controls." The student acknowledges immediately by saying, "I have the flight controls." The flight instructor again says, "You have the flight controls." When control is returned to the instructor, follow the same procedure. A visual check is recommended to verify that the exchange has occurred. There should never by any doubt as to who is flying the aircraft.

Metric Conversion Initiative

To assist pilots in understanding and using the metric measurement system, the practical test standards refer to the metric equivalent of various altitudes throughout. The inclusion of meters is intended to familiarize pilots with its use. The metric altimeter is arranged in 10 meter increments; therefore, when converting from feet to meters, the exact conversion, being too exact for practical purposes, is rounded to the nearest 10 meter increment or even altitude as necessary.

ADDITIONAL RATING TASK TABLE

	ADDITION OF A GLIDER RATING TO AN EXISTING PRIVATE PILOT CERTIFICATE							
AREA OF OPER- ATION	Required TASKS are indicated by either the TASK letter(s) that apply(s) or an indication that all or none of the TASKS must be tested.							
	ASEL	**ASES**	**AMEL**	**AMES**	**RH**	**RG**	**Balloon**	**Airship**
I	B,C,D	B,C,D	B,C,D	B,C,D	B,C,D	B,C,D	C,D	C,D
II	A,B,C,E	A,B,C,E	A,B,C,E	A,B,C,E	A,B,C,E	A,B,C,E	ALL	A,B,C,E
III	B	B	B	B	B	B	B	B
IV	ALL*	ALL*	ALL*	ALL*	ALL*	ALL*	ALL*	ALL*
V	ALL	ALL	ALL	ALL	ALL	ALL	ALL	ALL
VI	ALL	ALL	ALL	ALL	ALL	ALL	ALL	ALL
VII	ALL	ALL	ALL	ALL	ALL	ALL	ALL	ALL
VIII	NONE	NONE	NONE	NONE	NONE	NONE	A	NONE
IX	ALL	ALL	ALL	ALL	ALL	ALL	ALL	ALL
X	ALL	ALL	ALL	ALL	ALL	ALL	ALL	ALL
XI	ALL	ALL	ALL	ALL	ALL	ALL	ALL	ALL

*EXAMINER SHALL SELECT KIND OF LAUNCH BASED ON THE APPLICANT'S QUALIFICATIONS.

LEGEND

ASEL Airplane Single-Engine Land
ASES Airplane Single-Engine Sea
AMEL Airplane Multiengine Land
AMES Airplane Multiengine Sea
RH Rotorcraft Helicopter
RG Rotorcraft Gyroplane

APPLICANT'S PRACTICAL TEST CHECKLIST
Private Pilot—Glider

EXAMINER'S NAME _____
LOCATION _____
DATE/TIME _____

ACCEPTABLE AIRCRAFT

☐Aircraft Documents:
    Airworthiness Certificate
    Registration Certificate
    Operating Limitations
☐Aircraft Maintenance Records:
    Record of Airworthiness Inspections
    Current Status of Applicable Airworthiness Directives
Pilot's Operating Handbook, FAA-Approved Glider Flight Manual

PERSONAL EQUIPMENT

Practical Test Standard
Current Aeronautical Charts
Computer and Plotter
Flight Plan Form
Flight Log Form
Current AIM, Airport Facility Directory, and AppropriatePublications

PERSONAL RECORDS

Identification - Photo/Signature ID
Pilot Certificate
Completed FAA Form 8710-1, Airman Certificate and/or Rating Application with
    Instructor's Signature (if applicable)
Airman Test Report
Pilot Logbook with Appropriate Instructor Endorsements
FAA Form 8060-5, Notice of Disapproval (if applicable)
Approved School Graduation Certificate (if applicable)
Examiner's Fee (if applicable)

EXAMINER'S PRACTICAL TEST CHECKLIST
Private Pilot—Glider

APPLICANT'S NAME_____
LOCATION_____
DATE/TIME _____

I. PREFLIGHT PREPARATION
A. Certificates and Documents
B. Weather Information
C. Operation of Systems
D. Performance and Limitations
E. Aeromedical Factors

II. PREFLIGHT PROCEDURES
A. Assembly
B. Ground Handling
C. Preflight Inspection
D. Cockpit Management
E. Visual Signals

III. AIRPORT AND GLIDERPORT OPERATIONS
A. Radio Communications
B. Traffic Patterns
C. Airport, Runway, and Taxiway Signs, Markings, and Lighting

IV. LAUNCHES AND LANDINGS

AERO TOW
A. Before Takeoff Check
B. Normal and Crosswind Takeoff
C. Maintaining Tow Positions
D. Slack Line
E. Boxing The Wake
F. Tow Release
G. Abnormal Occurrences

GROUND TOW (AUTO OR WINCH)
H. Before Takeoff Check
I. Normal and Crosswind Takeoff
J. Abnormal Occurences

SELF-LAUNCH
K. Engine Starting
L. Taxiing
M. Before Takeoff Check
N. Normal and Crosswind Takeoff and Climb
O. Engine Shutdown In Flight
P. Abnormal Occurrences
204

LANDINGS

Q. Normal and Crosswind Landing

R. Slips to Landing

S. Downwind Landing

V. PERFORMANCE AIRSPEEDS

A. Minimum Sink Airspeed

B. Speed-To-Fly

VI. SOARING TECHNIQUES

A. Thermal Soaring

B. Ridge and Slope Soaring

C. Wave Soaring

VII. PERFORMANCE MANEUVERS

A. Straight Glides

B. Turns to Headings

C. Steep Turns

VIII. NAVIGATION

A. Flight Preparation and Planning

B. National Airspace System

IX. SLOW FLIGHT AND STALLS

A. Maneuvering at Minimum Control Airspeed

B. Stall Recognition and Recovery

X. EMERGENCY OPERATIONS

A. Simulated Off-Airport Landing

B. Emergency Equipment and Survival Gear

XI. POSTFLIGHT PROCEDURES

After-Landing and Securing

I. AREA OF OPERATION: PREFLIGHT PREPARATION

A. TASK: CERTIFICATES AND DOCUMENTS

REFERENCES: 14 CFR parts 43, 61, and 91; AC 61-23; Glider Flight Manual.

Objective. To determine that the applicant:

1. Exhibits knowledge of the elements related to certificates and documents by explaining—
   a. pilot certificate privileges and limitations.
   b. medical fitness.
   c. pilot logbook or flight records.

2. Exhibits knowledge of the elements related to certificates and documents by locating and explaining—
   a. airworthiness and registration certificates.
   b. operating limitations, placards, and instrument markings.
   c. weight and balance data and equipment list.
   d. maintenance requirements, appropriate records, airworthiness directives, and compliance records.

B. TASK: WEATHER INFORMATION

REFERENCES: AC 00-6, AC 00-45, AC 61-23, and AC 61-84; Soaring Flight Manual.

Objective. To determine that the applicant:

1. Exhibits knowledge of the elements related to weather information from various sources with emphasis on—
   a. use of weather reports, charts, and forecasts.
   b. significant weather prognostics.

2. Exhibits knowledge of the relationship of the following factors to the lifting process—
   a. pressure and temperature lapse rates.
   b. atmospheric instability.
   c. thermal index and thermal production.
   d. cloud formation and identification.
   e. frontal weather.
   f. other lifting sources.

3. Explains hazards associated with flight in the vicinity of thunderstorms.

4. Makes a competent "go/no-go" decision based on available weather information.

C. TASK: OPERATION OF SYSTEMS

REFERENCES: AC 61-23; Soaring Flight Manual, Glider Flight Manual.

Objective. To determine that the applicant:

1. Exhibits knowledge of the elements related to the operation of instruments and systems, including as appropriate—
a. magnetic compass.
b. yaw string or inclinometer.
c. airspeed indicator and altimeter.
d. variometer and total energy compensators.
e. gyroscopic instruments.
f. electrical.
g. landing gear and brakes.
h. avionics.
i. high-lift and drag devices.
j. oxygen equipment.

2. Correctly interprets information displayed on the instruments.

D. TASK: PERFORMANCE AND LIMITATIONS

REFERENCES: Soaring Flight Manual, Glider Flight Manual.

Objective. To determine that the applicant:

1. Exhibits knowledge of the elements related to performance and limitations, including the use of charts, tables, data to determine performance, and the adverse effects of exceeding limitations.
2. Uses appropriate performance charts, tables, and data.
3. Computes weight and balance, and determines if the weight and center of gravity are within limits.
4. Explains the management of ballast and its effect on performance.
5. Describes the effect of various atmospheric conditions on the glider's performance.
6. Explains the applicable performance speeds and their uses.
7. Describes the relationship between airspeeds and load factors.

E. TASK: AEROMEDICAL FACTORS

REFERENCES: AIM, Soaring Flight Manual.

Objective. To determine that the applicant exhibits knowledge of the elements related to aeromedical factors by explaining:

1. Symptoms, causes, effects, and corrective action of at least three (3) of the following—
a. hypoxia.
b. hyperventilation.
c. middle ear and sinus problems.
d. spatial disorientation.
e. motion sickness.
f. carbon monoxide poisoning (self-launch).
g. stress and fatigue.
h. dehydration and heatstroke.

2. Effects of alcohol and drugs, including over-the-counter drugs.

3. Effects of evolved gas from scuba diving on a pilot during flight.

II. AREA OF OPERATION: PREFLIGHT PROCEDURES

A. TASK: ASSEMBLY

NOTE: If, in the judgment of the examiner, the demonstration of the glider assembly is impractical, competency may be determined by oral testing.

REFERENCES: Soaring Flight Manual, Glider Flight Manual.

Objective. To determine that the applicant:

1. Exhibits knowledge of the elements related to assembly procedures.
2. Selects a suitable assembly area and provides sufficient crewmembers for assembly.
3. Follows an appropriate checklist.
4. Uses proper tools.
5. Handles components properly.
6. Cleans and lubricates parts, as appropriate.
7. Accounts for all tools and parts at the completion of assembly.
8. Performs post-assembly inspection, including a positive control check.

B. TASK: GROUND HANDLING

REFERENCES: Soaring Flight Manual, Glider Flight Manual.

Objective. To determine that the applicant:

1. Exhibits knowledge of the elements related to ground handling procedures.
2. Selects the appropriate ground handling procedures and equipment for existing conditions.
3. Determines the number of crewmembers needed.
4. Handles the glider in a manner that will not result in damage during movement.
5. Secures the glider and controls, as necessary, in proper position.

C. TASK: PREFLIGHT INSPECTION

REFERENCES: Soaring Flight Manual, Glider Flight Manual.

Objective. To determine that the applicant:

1. Exhibits knowledge of the elements related to preflight inspection, including which items must be inspected, for what reasons, and how to detect possible defects.
2. Inspects the glider using the appropriate checklist.
3. Verifies the glider is in condition for safe flight, notes any discrepancies, and determines if maintenance is required.
4. Inspects the launch equipment, including towline, tow hitches, weak links, and release mechanism.

D. TASK: COCKPIT MANAGEMENT

REFERENCES: 14 CFR part 91; Glider Flight Manual.

Objective. To determine that the applicant:

1. Exhibits knowledge of the elements related to cockpit management procedures.
2. Organizes and arranges material and equipment in a manner making items readily available.
3. Briefs passengers on the use of safety belts, shoulder harnesses, and emergency procedures.
4. Utilizes all appropriate checklists.

E. TASK: VISUAL SIGNALS

REFERENCE: Soaring Flight Manual.

Objective. To determine that the applicant:

1. Exhibits knowledge of the elements related to aero tow or ground tow visual signals, as appropriate.
2. Uses, interprets, and responds to prelaunch, launch, airborne, and emergency signals, as appropriate.

III. AREA OF OPERATION: AIRPORT AND GLIDERPORT OPERATIONS

A. TASK: RADIO COMMUNICATIONS

NOTE: If radio communications are impractical, competency may be determined by oral testing.

REFERENCE: AIM.

Objective. To determine that the applicant:

1. Exhibits knowledge of the elements related to radio communications, radio failure, and ATC light signals.
2. Selects appropriate frequencies for facilities to be used.
3. Transmits using recommended phraseology.
4. Acknowledges radio communications and complies with instructions.
5. Uses appropriate procedures for simulated radio communications failure.
6. Interprets and complies with ATC light signals.

B. TASK: TRAFFIC PATTERNS

REFERENCES: 14 CFR part 91; AC 90-66; Soaring Flight Manual.

Objective. To determine that the applicant:

1. Exhibits knowledge of the elements related to traffic pattern procedures for gliders.
2. Follows established traffic pattern procedures.
3. Maintains awareness of other traffic in pattern.
4. Maintains proper ground track with crosswind correction, if necessary.
5. Crosses designated points at appropriate altitudes, unless conditions make such action impractical.
6. Selects touchdown and stop points.
7. Adjusts glidepath and track promptly to compensate for unexpected lift, sink, or changes in wind velocity.
8. Makes smooth, coordinated turns with a bank angle not to exceed 45° when turning final approach.

9. Adjusts flaps, spoilers, or dive brakes, as appropriate.
10. Recognizes and makes appropriate corrections for the effect of wind.
11. Completes the prescribed checklist, if applicable.

C. TASK: AIRPORT, RUNWAY, AND TAXIWAY SIGNS, MARKINGS, AND LIGHTING

REFERENCES: AC 61-23; AIM.

Objective. To determine that the applicant:

1. Exhibits knowledge of the elements related to airport, runway, and taxiway signs, markings, and lighting.
2. Identifies, interprets, and complies with appropriate airport, runway, and taxiway signs, markings, and lighting.

IV. AREA OF OPERATION: LAUNCHES AND LANDINGS

NOTE: Examiner shall select kind of launch based on the applicant's qualifications.

AERO TOW

A. TASK: BEFORE TAKEOFF CHECK

REFERENCES: Soaring Flight Manual, Glider Flight Manual.

Objective. To determine that the applicant:

1. Exhibits knowledge of the elements related to the before takeoff check, including the reasons for checking the items, and how to detect malfunctions.
2. Establishes a course of action with crewmembers, including signals, speeds, wind, and emergency procedures.
3. Ensures that the glider is in safe operating condition.
4. Checks towline hookup and release mechanism, using the appropriate hook for the type of launch conducted.
5. Ensures no conflict with traffic prior to takeoff.
6. Completes the prescribed checklist, if applicable.

B. TASK: NORMAL AND CROSSWIND TAKEOFF

NOTE: If a crosswind condition does not exist, the applicant's knowledge of crosswind elements shall be evaluated through oral testing.

REFERENCES: Soaring Flight Manual, Glider Flight Manual.

Objective. To determine that the applicant:

1. Exhibits knowledge of the elements related to normal and crosswind takeoff, including configurations and tow positions.
2. Uses proper signals for takeoff.
3. Lifts off at an appropriate airspeed.
4. Maintains proper position until towplane lifts off.
5. Maintains directional control and proper wind-drift correction thoughout the takeoff.
6. Maintains proper alignment with the towplane.

C. TASK: MAINTAINING TOW POSITIONS

REFERENCE: Soaring Flight Manual.

Objective. To determine that the applicant:

1. Exhibits knowledge of the elements related to high-tow (slightly above the wake) and low-tow (slightly below the wake) positions during various phases of aero tow.
2. Makes smooth and correct control applications to maintain vertical and lateral positions during high and low tow.
3. Transitions from high- to low-tow position through the wake while maintaining positive control.
4. Maintains proper tow position during turns.

D. TASK: SLACK LINE

REFERENCE: Soaring Flight Manual.

Objective. To determine that the applicant:

1. Exhibits knowledge of the elements related to the causes, hazards, and corrections related to slack line.
2. Recognizes slack line and applies immediate, positive, and smooth corrective action to eliminate slack line in various situations.

E. TASK: BOXING THE WAKE

REFERENCE: Soaring Flight Manual.

Objective. To determine that the applicant:

1. Exhibits knowledge of the elements related to boxing the wake (maneuvering around the wake).
2. Maneuvers the glider, while on tow, slightly outside the towplane's wake in a rectangular, box-like pattern.
3. Maintains proper control and coordination.

F. TASK: TOW RELEASE

REFERENCE: Soaring Flight Manual.

Objective. To determine that the applicant:

1. Exhibits knowledge of the elements related to tow release, including related safety factors.
2. Maintains high-tow position with normal towline tension.
3. Clears the area before releasing the towline.
4. Releases the towline and confirms release by observing the towline.
5. Makes level or climbing turn.

G. TASK: ABNORMAL OCCURRENCES

REFERENCE: Soaring Flight Manual.

Objective. To determine that the applicant:

1. Exhibits knowledge of the elements related to aero tow abnormal occurrences, for various situations, such as —
a. towplane power loss during takeoff.
b. towline break.
c. towplane power failure at altitude.
d. glider release failure.
e. glider and towplane release failure.

2. Demonstrates simulated aero tow abnormal occurrences as required by the examiner.

GROUND TOW (AUTO OR WINCH)

H. TASK: BEFORE TAKEOFF CHECK

REFERENCES: Soaring Flight Manual, Glider Flight Manual.

Objective. To determine that the applicant:

1. Exhibits knowledge of the elements related to the before takeoff check, including the reasons for checking the items, and how to detect malfunctions.
2. Establishes a course of action with crewmembers, including signals, speeds, wind direction, and emergency procedures.
3. Ensures glider is in safe operating condition.
4. Checks towline hookup and release mechanism, using the appropriate hook for the type of launch conducted.
5. Ensures no conflict with traffic prior to takeoff.
6. Completes the prescribed checklist, if applicable.

I. TASK: NORMAL AND CROSSWIND TAKEOFF

NOTE: If a crosswind condition does not exist, the applicant's knowledge of crosswind elements shall be evaluated through oral testing.

REFERENCES: Soaring Flight Manual, Glider Flight Manual.

Objective. To determine that the applicant:

1. Exhibits knowledge of the elements related to normal and crosswind takeoff, including related safety factors.
2. Uses proper signals for takeoff.
3. Maintains directional control during launch.
4. Lifts off at the proper airspeed.
5. Establishes proper initial climb pitch attitude.
6. Takes prompt action to correct high speed, low speed, or porpoising.
7. Maintains proper ground track during climb.
8. Releases in proper manner and confirms release.

J. TASK: ABNORMAL OCCURRENCES

REFERENCES: Soaring Flight Manual, Glider Flight Manual.

Objective. To determine that the applicant:

1. Exhibits knowledge of the elements related to ground tow abnormal occurrences for various situations, such as —
a. overrunning the towline.
b. towline break.
c. inability to release towline.
d. over- and under-speeding.
e. porpoising.

2. Demonstrates simulated ground tow abnormal occurrences, as required by the examiner.

SELF-LAUNCH

K. TASK: ENGINE STARTING

REFERENCE: Glider Flight Manual

.

Objective. To determine that the applicant:

1. Exhibits knowledge of the elements related to engine starting, including various atmospheric conditions, and awareness of other persons and property during start.
2. Accomplishes recommended starting procedures.
3. Completes appropriate checklists.

L. TASK: TAXIING

REFERENCE: Glider Flight Manual.

Objective. To determine that the applicant:

1. Exhibits knowledge of the elements related to taxiing, including the effect of wind during taxiing and appropriate control positions.
2. Performs a brake check immediately after the glider begins moving.
3. Positions flight controls properly, considering the wind.
4. Controls direction and speed without excessive use of brakes.
5. Avoids other aircraft and hazards.
6. Complies with signals.

M. TASK: BEFORE TAKEOFF CHECK

REFERENCE: Glider Flight Manual.

Objective. To determine that the applicant:

1. Exhibits knowledge of the elements related to the before takeoff check, including the reason for checking each item and to detect malfunctions.
2. Positions the glider properly considering other aircraft, wind, and surface conditions.
3. Ensures engine temperatures and pressures are suitable for run-up and takeoff.
4. Accomplishes before takeoff checks and ensures the glider is in safe operating condition.
5. Reviews airspeeds, takeoff distance, and emergency procedures.
6. Completes appropriate checklists.

N. TASK: NORMAL AND CROSSWIND TAKEOFF AND CLIMB

NOTE: If a crosswind condition does not exist, the applicant's knowledge of crosswind elements shall be evaluated through oral testing.

REFERENCE: Glider Flight Manual.

Objective. To determine that the applicant:

1. Exhibits knowledge of the elements related to normal and crosswind takeoff and climb.
2. Positions flight controls for existing wind conditions.
3. Clears the area, taxies into takeoff position, and aligns the glider for departure.
4. Advances throttle smoothly to takeoff power.
5. Rotates at recommended airspeed, and accelerates to appropriate climb speed, +10/-5 knots.
6. Maintains takeoff power to a safe maneuvering altitude, then sets climb power.
7. Completes appropriate checklists.

O. TASK: ENGINE SHUTDOWN IN FLIGHT

REFERENCE: Glider Flight Manual.

Objective. To determine that the applicant:

1. Exhibits knowledge of the elements related to engine shutdown procedures in flight.
2. Sets power for proper engine cooling.
3. Establishes appropriate airspeed.
4. Sets electrical equipment.
5. Shuts down engine.
6. Feathers or positions propeller and stows, as applicable.
7. Selects proper static source, if applicable.
8. Completes appropriate checklists.

P. TASK: ABNORMAL OCCURRENCES

REFERENCES: Soaring Flight Manual, Glider Flight Manual.

Objective. To determine that the applicant:

1. Exhibits knowledge of the elements related to self-launch abnormal occurrences, for various situations, such as—
a. partial, complete power failure, and failure to gain restart.
b. fire or smoke.
c. electrical system malfunction.
d. low fuel pressure.
e. low oil pressure.
f. engine overheat.
g. canopy opening in flight.
h. engine restart in flight.

2. Demonstrates simulated self-launch abnormal occurrences, as required by the examiner.

LANDINGS

Q. TASK: NORMAL AND CROSSWIND LANDING

NOTE: If a crosswind condition does not exist, the applicant's knowledge of crosswind elements shall be evaluated through oral testing.

REFERENCES: Soaring Flight Manual, Glider Flight Manual.

Objective. To determine that the applicant:

1. Exhibits knowledge of the elements related to normal and crosswind approach and landing procedures.
2. Adjusts flaps, spoilers, or dive brakes, as appropriate.
3. Maintains recommended approach airspeed, +10/-5 knots.
4. Maintains crosswind correction and directional control throughout the approach and landing.
5. Makes smooth, timely, and positive control application during the roundout and touchdown.
6. Touches down smoothly within the designated landing area, with no appreciable drift, and with the longitudinal axis aligned with the desired landing path, stopping short of and within 200 feet (120 meters) of a designated point.
7. Maintains control during the after-landing roll.
8. Completes appropriate checklists.

R. TASK: SLIPS TO LANDING

REFERENCES: Soaring Flight Manual, Glider Flight Manual.

Objective. To determine that the applicant:

1. Exhibits knowledge of the elements related to forward, side, and turning slips to landing, with and without the use of drag devices.
2. Recognizes the situation where a slip should be used to land in a desired area.
3. Establishes a slip without the use of drag devices.
4. Maintains the desired ground track.
5. Maintains proper approach attitude.
6. Makes smooth, proper, and positive control applications during recovery from the slip.
7. Touches down smoothly within the designated landing area.

S. TASK: DOWNWIND LANDING

NOTE: This TASK may be evaluated orally at the discretion of the examiner.

REFERENCES: Soaring Flight Manual, Glider Flight Manual.

Objective. To determine that the applicant:

1. Exhibits knowledge of the elements related to downwind landings, including safety related factors.
2. Adjusts flaps, spoilers, or dive brakes, as appropriate.
3. Maintains recommended approach airspeed, ±5 knots.
4. Uses proper downwind landing procedures.
5. Maintains proper directional control during touchdown and roll-out.
6. Applies brake smoothly to bring glider to a stop.

V. AREA OF OPERATION: PERFORMANCE AIRSPEEDS

A. TASK: MINIMUM SINK AIRSPEED

REFERENCES: Soaring Flight Manual, Glider Flight Manual.

Objective. To determine that the applicant:

1. Exhibits knowledge of the elements related to aerodynamic factors and use of minimum sink airspeed.
2. Determines the minimum sink airspeed for a given situation and maintains the selected speed, ±5 knots.

218

B. TASK: SPEED-TO-FLY

REFERENCES: Soaring Flight Manual, Glider Flight Manual.

Objective. To determine that the applicant:

1. Exhibits knowledge of the elements related to speed-to-fly, and its uses.
2. Determines the speed-to-fly for a given situation and maintains the speed, ±5 knots.

VI. AREA OF OPERATION: SOARING TECHNIQUES

NOTE: Due to varying geographical locations and atmospheric conditions, the applicant may be asked to demonstrate at least one of the following soaring TASKS most appropriate for the particular location and existing conditions.

If conditions do not permit a demonstration of soaring skills, applicants will be expected to demonstrate knowledge of the various types of soaring through oral testing.

A. TASK: THERMAL SOARING

REFERENCE: Soaring Flight Manual.

Objective. To determine that the applicant:

1. Exhibits knowledge of the elements related to thermal soaring.
2. Recognizes the indications of, and the presence of, a thermal.
3. Analyzes the thermal structure and determines the direction to turn to remain within the thermal.
4. Exhibits coordinated control and planning when entering and maneuvering to remain within the thermal.
5. Applies correct techniques to re-enter the thermal, if lift is lost.
6. Remains oriented to ground references, wind, and other aircraft.
7. Maintains proper airspeeds in and between thermals.

B. TASK: RIDGE AND SLOPE SOARING

REFERENCE: Soaring Flight Manual.

Objective. To determine that the applicant:

1. Exhibits knowledge of the elements related to ridge and slope soaring.
2. Recognizes terrain features and wind conditions which create orographic lift.
3. Enters the area of lift properly.
4. Estimates height and maintains a safe distance from the terrain.
5. Exhibits smooth, coordinated control, and planning to remain within the area of lift.
6. Uses correct technique to re-enter the area of lift, if lift is lost.
7. Remains oriented to ground references, wind, and other aircraft.
8. Uses proper procedures and techniques when crossing ridges.
9. Maintains proper airspeeds.

C. TASK: WAVE SOARING

REFERENCE: Soaring Flight Manual.

Objective. To determine that the applicant:

1. Exhibits knowledge of the elements related to wave soaring.
2. Locates and enters the area of lift.
3. Exhibits smooth, coordinated control, and planning to remain within the area of lift.
4. Uses correct technique to re-enter the area of lift, if lift is lost.
5. Remains oriented to ground references, wind, and other aircraft.
6. Recognizes and avoids areas of possible extreme turbulence.
7. Maintains proper airspeeds.
8. Coordinates with ATC, as appropriate.

VII. AREA OF OPERATION: PERFORMANCE MANEUVERS

A. TASK: STRAIGHT GLIDES

REFERENCE: Soaring Flight Manual.

Objective. To determine that the applicant:

1. Exhibits knowledge of the elements related to straight glides, including the relationship of pitch attitude and airspeed.
2. Tracks toward a prominent landmark at a specified airspeed.
3. Demonstrates the effect of flaps, spoilers, or dive brakes, if equipped, in relation to pitch attitude and airspeed.
4. Exhibits smooth, coordinated control, and planning.
5. Maintains the specified heading, ±10°, and the specified airspeed, ±10 knots.

B. TASK: TURNS TO HEADINGS

REFERENCE: Soaring Flight Manual.

Objective. To determine that the applicant:

1. Exhibits knowledge of the elements related to turns to headings, including the relationship of pitch attitude, bank angle, and airspeed.
2. Enters and maintains an appropriate rate of turn with smooth, proper, and coordinated control applications.
3. Maintains the desired airspeed, ±10 knots, and rolls out on the specified heading, ±10°.

C. TASK: STEEP TURNS

REFERENCES: Soaring Flight Manual, Glider Flight Manual .

Objective. To determine that the applicant:

1. Exhibits knowledge of the elements related to steep turns, including load factor, effect on stall speed, and overbanking tendency.
2. Establishes the recommended entry airspeed.
3. Enters a turn maintaining a bank angle of 45°/±5°, with smooth and coordinated control applications.
4. Maintains desired airspeed, ±10 knots.
5. Recovers with smooth and coordinated control application within 10° of the desired heading.

VIII. AREA OF OPERATION: NAVIGATION

NOTE: The applicant's knowledge of this AREA OF OPERATION will be evaluated through oral testing.

A. TASK: FLIGHT PREPARATION AND PLANNING

REFERENCES: AC 61-23; AIM, Soaring Flight Manual.

Objective. To determine that the applicant:

1. Exhibits knowledge of the elements related to flight preparations and planning.
2. Selects and uses current and appropriate aeronautical charts.
3. Plots a course and selects prominent en route checkpoints .
4. Constructs a flight profile to determine minimum flight altitude at go-ahead points.
5. Explains method of using lift sources and speeds effectively within and between lift sources.
6. Selects available landing area.
7. Describes coordination procedures with air traffic control, as appropriate.

B. TASK: NATIONAL AIRSPACE SYSTEM

REFERENCES: 14 CFR part 91; AIM.

Objective. To determine that the applicant exhibits knowledge of the elements related to the National Airspace System by explaining:

1. Basic VFR weather minimums for all classes of airspace.
2. Airspace classes and their dimensions, pilot certification, and glider equipment requirements for the following—
   a. Class A.
   b. Class B.
   c. Class C.
   d. Class D.
   e. Class E.
   f. Class G.

3. Special use airspace and other airspace areas.

IX. AREA OF OPERATION: SLOW FLIGHT AND STALLS

A. TASK: MANEUVERING AT MINIMUM CONTROL AIRSPEED

REFERENCES: Soaring Flight Manual, Glider Flight Manual.

Objective. To determine that the applicant:

1. Exhibits knowledge of the elements related to maneuvering at minimum control airspeed, including flight characteristics and controllability.
2. Establishes and maintains the airspeed at which any further increase in angle of attack or change in configurations would result in a stall in straight or turning flight in various configurations and bank angles.
3. Adjusts the airspeed to avoid stalls in turbulent air or as bank is increased.
4. Applies control inputs in a smooth and coordinated manner.
5. Uses proper procedures to avoid stalls when raising a lowered wing.
6. Maintains heading, ±10°, during straight flight, and the desired bank angle, ±10°, during turns.

B. TASK: STALL RECOGNITION AND RECOVERY

REFERENCES: Soaring Flight Manual, Glider Flight Manual.

Objective. To determine that the applicant:

1. Exhibits knowledge of the elements related to stall recognition and recovery, including the aerodynamic factors and flight situations that may result in stalls, and the hazards of stalling during uncoordinated flight.

2. Selects an entry altitude that will allow the maneuver to be completed no lower than 1,500 feet AGL.
3. Establishes and maintains a pitch attitude that will result in a stall during both straight and turning flight with and without flaps, spoilers, or dive brakes, as appropriate.
4. Maintains a specified bank angle of up to 15° of bank, ±10°, during turns.
5. Recovers at the stall.
6. Uses smooth and coordinated control applications throughout the maneuver.

X. AREA OF OPERATION: EMERGENCY OPERATIONS

NOTE: These TASKS are knowledge only.

A. TASK: SIMULATED OFF-AIRPORT LANDING

REFERENCES: Soaring Flight Manual, Glider Flight Manual.

Objective. To determine that the applicant exhibits knowledge of the elements related to a simulated off-airport landing, including selection of a suitable landing area and the procedures used to accomplish an off-airport landing.

B. TASK: EMERGENCY EQUIPMENT AND SURVIVAL GEAR

REFERENCES: Soaring Flight Manual, Glider Flight Manual .

Objective. To determine that the applicant exhibits knowledge of the elements related to emergency equipment and survival gear, appropriate to the glider used for the practical test, by describing:

1. Location in the glider.
2. Method of operation or use.
3. Servicing and storage.
4. Inspection, fitting, and use of parachutes.
5. Equipment and gear appropriate for operation in various climates and over various types of terrain.

XI. AREA OF OPERATION: POSTFLIGHT PROCEDURES

TASK: AFTER-LANDING AND SECURING

REFERENCES: Soaring Flight Manual, Glider Flight Manual .

Objective. To determine that the applicant:

1. Exhibits knowledge of the elements related to after-landing and securing procedures, including local and ATC operations, ramp safety, parking hand signals, shutdown (if appropriate), securing, and postflight inspection.
2. Selects a suitable parking area while considering wind and safety of nearby persons and property.
3. Taxies to parking area and performs engine shutdown, if applicable.
4. Services the glider, if applicable.
5. Secures the glider properly.
6. Performs a satisfactory postflight inspection.
7. Completes the prescribed checklist.

Index

G

G loads 116
glide path control 62
glide ratio 66
GLIDER, COMMERCIAL RATING 2
Gold Badge 187
Gust load factor 117

H

high tow position 36

I

INDUCED DRAG 11
INSTRUMENTATION 16
INTERFERENCE DRAG 12

L

L/D 106
landing pattern 62
lateral axis 12
Lazy 8 180
Lee Wave 141
leveling data 121
lift 8
limit load factors 116
load factor 116
longitudinal axi 12
low tow position 51

M

max L/D 106
Maximum Design airspeed 120
Maximum Design Speed 105
MEAN AERODYNAMIC CHORD 122
minimum sinking speed 76, 105
MOMENT 122

N

negative 'G's 84
negative load factors 118
netto 19
Never Exceed speed 120

O

OAR 23
obstructions 154
off field landings 149
overshooting 64
oxygen systems 142

P

PARASITE DRAG 11
Part 61.87 1
Part 830 1
part 91 1
polar 105
positive control check 25
Power lines 155
pre-landing checklist 62
preflight checklist 25
preflight inspection 23
premature termination of the tow 52
prop wash 36
PT3 52

R

registration certificate 24
Reichmann 149
RELATIVE NETTO 19
release knob 39
requirements for the private glider flight
    test 1
Ridge soaring 137
ridge soaring rules 139
rope breaks 54
rudder 5
running their wing 48

S

Sailplane and Gliding 149
secondary stall 84
shudder 82
sideslip 13, 100
Silver Badge 187
Silver distance 150

slack in the rope 40
slip 70, 98
slip-skid indicator 6
Soaring Society Of America 184
speed-to-fly 103
speed-to-fly directors 19
speed-to-fly ring 111
spin 93
spiral dive 96
SPIRAL INSTABILITY 14
spoiler 7
SSA 149
stability 12
stall 80
stall recovery, 81
Standing Wave 141
steep approaches 67
steep turns 75
stick thermals 18
Super Netto 19

T

tail wind 59
That Looks About Right 63
thermalling airspeed 130
thermalling altitude limits 68
Thermals 127
thermistors 18
TLAR 63
total energy 18
total energy probe 18
touchdown 67
touchdown point 62
tow pilot 60
tow rope 34
turning stall 86

U

unassisted takeoff 46
USEFUL LOAD 122
USTAL 62

V

variometer 17
vertical axis 12

W

Wave 141
weight and balance 26
Wilber Wright 6
winch launching 53
Wind gradient 73
wind sock 74
Wing loading 77
wing runner 34
wires 155
WRITTEN TEST 3

Y

yaw string 6
yellow triangle 17

BIBLIOGRAPHY

AFTER SOLO by Thomas Knauff, Julian Pa., 3rd edition (1996)

FLIGHT TRAINING HANDBOOK by the FAA AC 61-21A, US Government Printing Office, Wash D.C.(1980)

FLIGHT TRAINING HANDBOOK by Jeppesen Sanderson inc., Denver Col, and The Soaring Society of America, Los Angeles Cal (1978)

GLIDER BASICS FROM FIRST FLIGHT TO SOLO by Thomas Knauff, Julian Pa., 7th edition (1998)

GLIDING by Derek Piggott, 7th edition Knauff & Grove (1997)

NEW SOARING PILOT by Welch and Irving, 3rd edition Pitman Press, Bath England (1977)

OFF FIELD LANDINGS by Tom Knauff (1996)

PRIVATE GLIDER PILOT PRACTICAL TEST STANDARDS FAA-S-8-81-22 by the Federal Aviation Agency

RIDGE SOARING THE BALD EAGLE RIDGE by Thomas Knauff, Julian Pa., 4th edition (1995)

SOARING CROSS COUNTRY by Helmut Reichmann, 1st edition Thomson Publications USA (1980)

STICK AND RUDDER by Wolfgang Langeweisch, 1st edition McGraw Hill Publishing New York (1944 & 1972)

THE GLIDER FLYING HANDBOOK By Thomas Knauff 2007 (Reprint of FAA manual with numerous improvements, and corrections.)

UNDERSTANDING GLIDING by Derek Piggott, 3rd edition Adam & Charles Black, London (1990)